MARY'S

Foolproof Dinners

MARY'S

Foolproof Dinners

120 effortless recipes from my brand-new BBC series

BBC BOOKS

Contents

———

Introduction

Welcome to my latest book *Foolproof Dinners*. What does 'dinner' mean to you? To me, it is the main meal of the day, whether that is lunch or in the evening, a supper or a more special occasion. I have focussed on the main meal of the day because, with that meal sorted, the rest of the day will follow.

I always think of myself as a teacher, and I want to share the knowledge that I have gathered over the years. This is why I like to explain every process clearly so the recipes are foolproof for you, the home cook. We've included instructions that are a little bit more detailed, so that you have success every time. As life gets busier, we take more short cuts – I never make puff or filo pastry any more, and if I haven't any stock, I use a stock pot. These compromises make sense when the ready-prepared products are so good. In this way and others, we aim to simplify the method, wherever possible.

I feel there's no use having fancy tins or dishes that only come out of the cupboard once a year, and the same goes for ingredients. I have incorporated some flavours that are new to me, like sriracha (see pages 93 and 196), but I've made sure they don't just feature once. Other combinations, like chimichurri, use familiar ingredients, but in an interesting and different way. When all the family come round, serving something comforting but rich, like the Coq au Vin Pie (see page 95), will always be a hit. Or try the Three Fish and Potato Gratin (see page 64), which is quicker than a standard version, as it has no mashed potato on top, but is equally delicious. More and more I like recipes that can be made all in one dish to bake, like the Slow-cooked Spiced Lamb (see page 123), or are cooked in one pan on the hob, like the Prawn Fried Rice with Vegetables (see page 46). These save on washing up, as well as being easy to serve.

Enjoy the recipes, make your own notes in the margins or write post-it notes and stick them on the page as a reminder to yourself of which dish you used, for example, or who you served the recipe to. Next time, you won't have to think. I love a well-used book!

Mary Berry

Cook's Notes

Here are some general guides that will help make your cooking foolproof.
Cooking does not need to be stressful and can be easy and simple,
and I feel it's important to enjoy preparing your meals so the process
of sharing food with friends and family is even more special.

Read the recipe

I always suggest you read the recipe all the
way through to the end before starting to
cook. That way, you can make sure you have
all the correct equipment – the right size
tin or a lid for the pan – before you start,
and that the oven is set to the right
temperature and all the ingredients are
weighed accurately. This is so important.

Oven and grill temperatures

As ovens and grills vary in the amount of
heat they produce, you may need to cook a
dish for slightly longer or shorter than the
recipe states. It can be helpful to use an oven
thermometer to find out how accurate your
oven is.

Metric and imperial

I have provided both metric and imperial
measurements. It's best to stick to one or
the other when you are following a recipe
– particularly if you are baking. Spoon
measurements are level measuring spoons,
unless otherwise stated.

Tins and equipment

Use the size of tins and dishes I suggest,
otherwise the food can cook differently.
If your roasting tin, for example, is slightly
larger than I recommend, the liquid may
evaporate more quickly and the sauce may
be too thick. Conversely, if your tin is smaller,
it will cook more slowly and the sauce may
be too runny. It is especially important to
use the correct size tin when baking cakes.

Scales and measuring spoons

I find digital scales really are the best and
the most accurate. Years ago, digital ones
weren't accurate but everything is much more
efficient now. Balance scales can vary slightly,
especially if they have been knocked or the
balance is slightly off centre. Do check each
time before weighing. Another essential
kitchen item is a set of measuring spoons for
measuring baking powder, spices and small
amounts of liquids.

Ovenproof pans and flameproof casseroles

A number of my recipes for savoury stews and one-pan dishes begin on the hob and are then cooked in the oven. I tend to use large, deep frying pans, as the ones I have at home are ovenproof, but it would be just as good to use a flameproof casserole. So long as it has a lid that fits and is suitable to use on the hob and in the oven, it will do the job.

Eggs

Use free-range large chicken eggs, unless otherwise stated.

Free-range meat

Buy the best-quality meat you can afford. British farmers have some of the highest food standards in the world and it really does make a difference. Animals should be looked after and loved, fed properly and regularly, and respected for the nourishment they provide. I always use free-range chicken. Venison is having a little resurgence as a lean, tender meat. We have included two recipes on pages 129–30.

Sustainable fish

Buy fish that is sustainably sourced. It will advertise itself as such on the packet, or ask at the fish counter in your local supermarket or check with your fishmonger. The levels of fish stocks do change, though, so while I have tried to ensure all the recipes include fish that are on the sustainability list, do swap one for another if necessary.

Vegetables

Use medium-sized vegetables, unless otherwise stated.

Vegetarian and vegan recipes

More and more often, I will choose to cook without meat at home. I have included a wide variety of vegetarian dishes and they are some of my favourite recipes in the book – Lasagne Aubergine Melanzane (see page 157) and Leek and Gruyère Tart with Parmesan and Chive Pastry (see page 162) are great for cooking ahead when friends come round, and Spiced Aubergine and Fresh Tomato Spaghetti (see page 143) is a quick midweek supper.

Cauliflowers and cabbage are very much a staple ingredient in plant-based cooking. Back in the day, these were unpopular and fairly soggy vegetables but they now take centre stage in many dishes we cook – see Chargrilled Pointed Cabbage with Tomato Dressing (page 196) and Cauliflower and Sweet Potato Curry (page 154).

Slaws

We have included three slaws in this book – Sweet Potato and Celeriac Slaw (see page 180), Lemon and Chive Coleslaw (see page 178) and Brussels Sprout, Celeriac and Horseradish Slaw (see page 183). They are a healthy and adventurous way to serve a variety of vegetables, offering diverse nutritional values for the family. Different dressings give a choice of flavours and they can be used to accompany many dishes.

Flavours

With each new book, I try to incorporate a few flavours that are new to me. We use them in the recipes to change a classic or create a fresh idea with interesting flavours and aromas. Here we have used Sriracha, which is a chilli sauce that is new to me but is very popular, especially with teenagers. Try the Sriracha Chicken Wings on page 93.

We have also included our adaptation of the Uruguayan/Argentinian herby Chimichurri sauce. This is great for marinades or to serve on the side. It keeps in the fridge and goes well with cold meat or the pork fillet on page 107.

The spiced lamb recipe on page 123 brings together some traditional Lebanese flavours – cinnamon, allspice and coriander.

I have been using miso paste for a few years, but it is worth a mention here. Miso is a Japanese protein-based savoury flavouring made from fermented steamed soya beans. It is available as red, white, yellow or red/brown miso paste, though our favourite is white. It is used to give depth and body, and when used as a marinade adds lots of flavour.

Foolproof Tips

Ovens and grills

It is so important to make sure that the very first thing you do when you are cooking is preheat the oven or grill, especially with baking, as cooking at an accurate temperature is imperative. A slight change in temperature will affect the look, rise and texture of a bake.

Preparing ahead

I like to do some preparation ahead of time, especially when I have people coming round. I have included instructions on how to get ahead with all the recipes that can be.

Baking tins and oven dishes

Measure the diameter and volume of all your roasting tins, baking tins and oven dishes and write the size on the bottoms. You will quickly be able to find the right tin or dish for the job when you come to need one later on. It is so important to use the correct size of dish, too. If you use something too big, you might find the food is overcooked and if you use something too small, you might find it undercooked or spilling out.

Freezer

If you are worried about slicing a terrine or a cold tart or mousse (for example, the Chocolate Truffle Tart on page 214), the trick is to get it really cold first. I will sometimes put a dish in the freezer for half an hour to firm up before slicing, so the cut is clean.

Meat and fish

If you are cooking multiple fillets, or are cutting the meat up into cubes for a stew, make sure they are all an equal size. This will ensure they all cook at the same rate and you aren't left with some under-done and others over-done.

Mussels and clams

If any mussels or clams are open before cooking, give them a tap. If they close, they are fine; if not, discard them. Likewise discard any that are still closed after cooking. If you can't find 'ready-to-cook' mussels, place the fresh mussels in a large bowl of cold water and scrub to clean them. Remove any beards, which are the stringy threads on the side of the shell, and discard any broken mussels or any that stay open after being tapped.

Pastry lids

If you are cooking a pie, it is important to make a hole in the lid to allow the steam to escape and prevent the pastry from becoming soggy. Also, if the dish is deep, you may need to use a pie funnel or small teacup in the centre (put this in place before you add the filling and top with the pastry); this prevents the pastry from sinking down and touching the surface of the filling, which can make it soggy.

Dinner for two

Recipes for kids

To Begin With

Guacamole and Hot-smoked Salmon Canapés

Hot-smoked salmon is smokier than traditional smoked salmon and the texture is different, too. It flakes beautifully and is wonderful on top of these canapés.

Makes 20–25

3 tortilla wraps, each cut into 8 triangles

2 tbsp olive oil

1 large avocado, mashed

½ small red onion, finely chopped

1 garlic clove, finely grated

½ bunch of coriander, leaves finely chopped

1 large tomato, deseeded and finely chopped

Juice of ½ large lime

¼ red chilli, deseeded and finely chopped (optional)

75g (3oz) hot-smoked salmon, flaked

Mary's Tips

Triangles can be made 4 hours ahead. Best assembled to serve.

Not suitable for freezing.

1. Preheat the oven to 200°C/180°C Fan/Gas 6.

2. Brush both sides of the triangles with oil and sprinkle with salt. Place on a large baking sheet and bake in the oven for about 12 minutes or until golden and crisp. Set aside to cool.

3. Place the avocado, onion, garlic, coriander, tomato, lime juice and chilli, if using, in a bowl. Season well with salt and freshly ground black pepper and mix together.

4. Spoon a small amount of the guacamole onto each triangle, then top with a flake of salmon.

5. Arrange on a platter to serve.

Chilled Watercress and Cucumber Soup

**Perfect as a refreshing and chilled first course on a
balmy evening. Serve it with chunky bread.**

Serves 4

2 tbsp sunflower oil

2 large onions, sliced

750ml (1¼ pints)
   chicken stock

175g (6oz) frozen
   petits pois

150g (5oz) watercress,
   coarsely chopped

1 large cucumber,
   peeled and
   diced (keep one
   piece of peel)

½ tsp caster sugar

Mary's Tips

*The best way to remove
the seeds from the
cucumber is to slice
the cucumber in half
lengthways, then slide
a teaspoon down the
middle. Soup can be
made up to a day ahead.*

Freezes well.

1. Heat the oil in a large saucepan over a high heat. Add the onions and fry for about 10 minutes until starting to soften.

2. Pour in the stock and bring up to the boil. Add the frozen petits pois, cover with a lid and simmer for about 3–4 minutes. Remove from the heat, add the watercress and stir until wilted. Set aside to cool.

3. Add the diced cucumber and sugar to the cooled soup and season with lots of salt and freshly ground black pepper. Using a stick blender or food processor, purée until smooth.

4. Chill in the fridge until ready to serve. Meanwhile, take the reserved piece of cucumber skin and slice it into very thin slivers about 2cm (¾in) long.

5. Divide the soup between four bowls and add a sprinkling of cucumber strips to each one to serve.

Haddock, Prawn and Sweetcorn Chowder

**A warming, hearty and delicious soup, this is easy and quick to make.
A meal in its own right, this is perfect for lunch with crusty bread.**

Serves 4–6

55g (2oz) butter

2 banana shallots, diced

2 sticks celery,
thinly sliced

1 carrot, peeled
and diced

3 tbsp plain flour

450ml (¾ pint)
fish stock

450ml (¾ pint)
full-fat milk

200g (7oz) potatoes,
peeled and cut into
3cm (1¼in) dice

300g (10½oz) smoked
haddock, skinned
and cut into 3cm
(1¼in) dice

175g (6oz) raw prawns

115g (4oz) tinned
sweetcorn, drained

2 tbsp freshly chopped
parsley, to serve

Mary's Tips

*Can be made up to
8 hours ahead. Add
haddock, prawns
and sweetcorn
when reheating.*

Not suitable for freezing.

1. Melt the butter in a saucepan over a medium–high heat.
   Add the shallots, celery and carrot and fry for 3–4 minutes.
   Sprinkle in the flour and stir for a few seconds. Blend in the
   stock, then the milk, stirring until thickened.

2. Add the potatoes, cover with a lid and simmer over a low
   heat for about 8 minutes, until the potatoes are just cooked.

3. Add the smoked haddock, raw prawns and sweetcorn and
   simmer for 5 minutes, until the prawns have turned pink.
   Season well with a little salt and some freshly ground
   black pepper.

4. Sprinkle with the parsley and serve piping hot in wide bowls.

Courgette and Blue Cheese Soup

This soup tastes like a real treat – a hug in a bowl. It's a great recipe for using up any excess home-grown courgettes. Best not to use marrow, though, as it contains a lot more water and will make the soup taste insipid.

Serves 4–6

Large knob of butter

3 small leeks, thinly sliced

1 garlic clove, finely grated

750g (1lb 10oz) courgettes, sliced into rounds

3 tbsp plain flour

1 litre (1¾ pints) hot vegetable stock

175g (6oz) Stilton or firm blue cheese, grated

3 tbsp freshly chopped parsley

Mary's Tips

Can be made up to 8 hours ahead.

Freezes well.

1. Melt the butter in a deep saucepan over a high heat. Add the leeks and fry for a few minutes. Add the garlic and courgettes and fry for 3 minutes.

2. Sprinkle in the flour and stir to coat the vegetables. Gradually pour in the stock, stirring well until the soup comes to a boil. Cover with a lid, reduce the heat and simmer gently for about 15 minutes, until all the vegetables are soft.

3. Remove the pan from the heat and, using a stick blender or food processor, blend the soup until smooth. Pour back into a pan and return to the heat. Add the Stilton or firm blue cheese and stir until melted. Season well with salt and freshly ground black pepper.

4. Pour into warm bowls, sprinkle with the chopped parsley and serve with chunky bread.

Roast Chicken Soup

When you are feeling like comfort food or are a little under the weather, this is the go-to soup. Hearty and warming. Buy fat chicken wings with meat on, not just the tips. Using chicken stock as well as the stock from the simmered chicken wings makes a wonderful soup.

Serves 6

500g (1lb 2oz)
   chicken wings
2 carrots
5 sticks celery
2 large onions,
   unpeeled and
   quartered
5 bay leaves
2 litres (3½ pints)
   good chicken stock

Mary's Tips

*Can be made up
to a day ahead.*

Freezes well.

1. Preheat the oven to 220°C/200°C Fan/Gas 7.

2. Place the chicken wings in a roasting tin and roast in the preheated oven for 35–40 minutes until golden brown and cooked through.

3. Slice 1 carrot and 3 sticks of celery into pieces and place in the pan with the quartered onions. Add the browned chicken wings, bay leaves and chicken stock. Cover with a lid and bring up to the boil. Reduce the heat and simmer gently for 30 minutes. Remove the lid and continue to simmer for another 30 minutes.

4. Meanwhile, cut the remaining carrot and celery into small dice about the size of a pea.

5. Drain the soup through a colander into a clean saucepan, making sure to push all the liquid into the pan. Remove the chicken meat from the wings and set aside. Discard the bones and cooked veg. Add the diced carrot and celery and chicken meat to the soup and bring to the boil. Simmer for 5 minutes.

6. Spoon into warm bowls to serve.

Spiced Roasted Cashews

A tasty alternative to crisps before supper. These make a nice gift, too – just place in a small Kilner jar and add a nice label and ribbon.

Makes 400g
(14oz)

400g (14oz) plain
  cashew nuts
2 tbsp sunflower oil
2 tbsp sweet smoked
  paprika
1 tsp ground cumin
½ tsp dried chilli flakes
1 tsp sea salt flakes

Mary's Tips

*Can be made up
to a day ahead.*

Not suitable for freezing.

1. Preheat the oven to 180°C/160°C Fan/Gas 4.

2. Scatter the cashews onto a large baking sheet, drizzle the oil over the top and sprinkle over the spices and chilli. Season well with freshly ground black pepper and toss together to coat. Roast in the preheated oven for about 15–20 minutes, turning from time to time.

3. Remove from the oven, sprinkle with the sea salt flakes and leave to cool.

Salmon and Dill Pickle Bites

Just like a mini sausage roll but with a salmon and herb mixture in the centre. Always serve these warm – they are great with drinks or would make a lovely light meal with a fresh salad. These are little bites but you could make them longer, if you wish.

Makes 24

1 × 320g sheet ready-rolled all-butter puff pastry
1 egg, beaten

For the filling
200g (7oz) salmon fillet, skinned and finely diced
115g (4oz) smoked salmon, finely chopped
125g (5oz) full-fat cream cheese
25g (1oz) Parmesan, finely grated
Small bunch of dill, finely chopped
6 spring onions, trimmed and finely chopped
Juice of ½ lemon
75g (3oz) dill pickle from a jar, finely chopped

Mary's Tips

Can be made up to 3 days ahead and reheated to serve.

The uncooked bites freeze well.

1. Preheat the oven to 200°C/180°C Fan/Gas 6. Place a large baking sheet in the oven to get hot.

2. Place all the filling ingredients in a large bowl. Mix well and season with salt and freshly ground black pepper.

3. Unroll the pastry on a lightly floured work surface and roll out to a large rectangle about 30 × 40cm (12 × 16in). Have the long edge nearest to you. Brush the surface with some beaten egg. Cut the pastry vertically into three even pieces.

4. Divide the filling mixture into three. Using one piece of pastry, place a third of the mixture in a mound along the length of it. Lift and fold the pastry over to seal the filling. Seal the edge using the back of a fork. Repeat with the remaining mixture and pastry to make three rolls.

5. Slice each section into 8 and brush the tops with beaten egg. Carefully remove the hot baking sheet from the oven, line with non-stick baking paper and place the rolls on top. Bake in the preheated oven for about 18–20 minutes until golden brown.

6. Serve warm.

Burrata with Tomato and Cucumber Salsa

A delicious first course or a lovely addition to a sharing platter. It is essential that all the salsa ingredients are diced into tiny, pea-sized pieces. My favourite pitted black olives are semi-dried in a packet.

Serves 2–3 as a sharing dish

½ part-baked ciabatta, sliced into 8 or 9 (approximately 135g/4¾oz)

2 tbsp olive oil, plus extra to finish

1 burrata ball (approximately 150g/5oz)

Balsamic glaze, to finish

For the salsa

150g (5oz) cherry tomatoes, diced

½ cucumber, peeled, deseeded and diced

25g (1oz) pitted black olives, diced

2 tsp white wine vinegar

2 tbsp finely chopped fresh basil

2 tbsp olive oil

Mary's Tips

Salsa can be made up to 6 hours ahead.

Not suitable for freezing

1. Preheat the oven to 220°C/200°C Fan/Gas 7.

2. Brush both sides of each slice of ciabatta with olive oil. Place them on a baking sheet and bake for about 10–12 minutes, until golden and crisp. Set aside.

3. Place the tomatoes, cucumber, olives, vinegar, basil and olive oil in a small bowl and mix well. Season with salt and freshly ground black pepper.

4. Spoon three quarters of the salsa into the centre of a serving plate and spread out slightly with the back of a spoon. Place the burrata on top in the centre of the plate. Break the burrata and spoon the remaining salsa over the top.

5. Arrange the ciabatta around the edges of the plate. Drizzle the burrata and salsa with balsamic glaze and some more olive oil before serving.

Poker Chips

Delicious cheese and olive biscuits, so quick and easy to make. We always use all-butter puff pastry; it can be trickier to handle than the one without all-butter, as it becomes soft especially in a warm kitchen, but just keep it in the fridge in between slicing. Buy black olive tapenade in jars from the deli counter in good supermarkets.

Makes 28–32

1 × 320g sheet ready-rolled all-butter puff pastry

2 tbsp black olive tapenade

55g (2oz) mature Cheddar, grated

1 egg, beaten

55g (2oz) Parmesan, grated

Mary's Tips

Can be made up to a day ahead. Reheat until warm to serve.

Freeze well.

1. Unroll the pastry onto a lightly floured work surface. Spread the tapenade over one half of the pastry. Sprinkle the Cheddar on top of the tapenade, then fold the other side of the pastry over like a book to enclose the cheese and tapenade.

2. Dust the top of the pastry with a little flour and reroll to its original rectangular size and shape. Brush the surface with beaten egg and sprinkle with the Parmesan. Very gently roll the rolling pin over the top to press the cheese into the pastry. Transfer the pastry to the fridge and chill for about 30 minutes.

3. Preheat the oven to 200°C/180°C Fan/Gas 6. Line 2 baking sheets with non-stick baking paper.

4. Trim the edges of the rectangle to make them neat, if needed, then divide the pastry into 4 strips vertically. Remove a small triangle from each end (these can be cook's treats!), then slice each strip into diamond shapes. You should get about 6–7 diamonds out of each strip. Chill in the fridge for 10 minutes to firm up.

5. Place the diamonds and triangles on the prepared baking sheets and bake in the preheated oven for about 15 minutes, or until pale golden brown on top and underneath. Leave to cool slightly on a wire rack.

6. Serve warm.

Artichoke and Chive Dip

This is so moreish and something quite different. Perfect as a dip or on a sharing platter. The longer it is left in the fridge, the more the flavours infuse.

Serves 6

115g (4oz) full-fat
  mayonnaise
200g (7oz) full-fat
  crème fraîche
Juice of ½ lemon
75g (3oz) mature
  Cheddar, grated
30g (1oz) Parmesan,
  grated
½ small red onion,
  roughly chopped
2 garlic cloves,
  finely grated
1 × 400g tin artichoke
  hearts, drained
2 tbsp finely
  snipped chives

Mary's Tips

*Can be made up
to a day ahead.*

Not suitable for freezing.

1. Measure all the ingredients, except for the chives, into a food processor. Add salt and freshly ground black pepper and whiz until blended. Check the seasoning and spoon into a bowl.

2. Sprinkle with the snipped chives and serve with crudités or toasted pitta.

Weekend Sharing Platter

The perfect sharing platter for lunch or supper – an easy fish pâté, baked Camembert and sides. We love these baked tortillas, which are easy and delicious, but you could have crusty bread, toasted pitta or baguette, if preferred.

Serves 6–8

2 large tortilla wraps
2 tbsp olive oil
1 whole Camembert
Sprig of rosemary
1 garlic clove, sliced
    into thin slivers
3 sticks celery, sliced
    into thin batons

For the sardine pâté

1 × 135g tin sardines in
    oil, drained well
55g (2oz) soft butter
75g (3oz) full-fat
    cream cheese
Juice of 1 lemon
½ bunch of basil, leaves
    finely chopped

For the tomato salsa

350g (12oz) ripe tomatoes,
    deseeded and cut into
    pea-sized pieces
½ small red onion, diced
½ bunch of basil, leaves
    finely chopped
3 tbsp olive oil
1 tbsp balsamic glaze

Mary's Tips

Pâté can be made a day ahead.

Not suitable for freezing.

1. Preheat the oven to 200°C/180°C Fan/Gas 6. Line a large baking sheet with non-stick baking paper.

2. Using scissors, cut each wrap in half, then snip into medium-sized triangles. Brush both sides with olive oil and season well with salt and freshly ground black pepper. Spread out onto the prepared baking sheet. Bake in the preheated oven for about 10–12 minutes, until pale golden brown. Set aside to cool and crispen on the baking sheet.

3. To make the pâté, remove the centre bone from the drained sardines and discard. Put the sardines in a small bowl and mash coarsely with a fork. Stir in the butter. Add all the remaining ingredients and season well. Mix until combined but still with a little texture. Spoon into a serving bowl and leave to chill in the fridge.

4. For the salsa, place all the ingredients in a bowl and mix well. Season, then spoon into a small serving bowl.

5. Remove the Camembert from its wrapper and place in a shallow ovenproof dish. Separate the sprig of rosemary into small pieces and insert into the top of the cheese with the garlic slivers. Bake in the preheated oven for about 5–10 minutes, until warm and starting to melt in the centre.

6. Place the cheese, pâté and salsa on a large board or platter. Put the celery batons in a small glass tumbler and place next to the cheese. Scatter the tortilla wedges around the board to serve.

Gardener's Delight

Fresh and delicious, this is ideal as a first course. I don't usually skin tomatoes but it is worth it for this salad. The crème fraîche and pesto make a lovely sauce. Serve on individual plates, if liked, but for a change we serve this in small, shallow, pasta-type bowls.

Makes 4

6 large ripe tomatoes

1 large ripe avocado

4 heaped tbsp
   crème fraîche

3 tbsp fresh green pesto

12 cherry tomatoes,
   halved

200g (7oz) small
   mozzarella balls

Small bunch of basil

Balsamic glaze,
   to finish

Olive oil, to finish

Mary's Tips

Can be assembled up to an hour ahead. Skin tomatoes up to 6 hours ahead.

Not suitable for freezing.

1. To skin the tomatoes, bring a pan of water to the boil. Make a cross in the base of the tomatoes and add them to the pan. Simmer for about 30 seconds, until the skin is loosened, then drain and place in a bowl of cold water. When they are cool enough to handle, peel the skin and trim the end. Slice the tomatoes into thick slices.

2. Peel the avocado and cut into thin slices.

3. Spread 1 heaped tablespoon of crème fraîche into the base of 4 shallow bowls. Spread 1 heaped teaspoon of pesto on top and season with salt and freshly ground black pepper. Arrange slices of tomato on top of each bowl. Divide the avocado between the sliced tomatoes and top with the cherry tomato halves.

4. Place the remaining pesto in a small bowl, add the mozzarella balls and toss to coat. Divide the balls between the bowls.

5. Garnish each bowl with a few basil leaves and a drizzle of balsamic glaze and olive oil. Season well with rock salt and freshly ground black pepper before serving.

Garlic and Tomato Ciabatta

**These are loved by everyone. It's easy to adapt the recipe, too,
and add other flavours, such as grated cheese or olive tapenade.
Good to hand round with drinks outside on a fine day.**

Serves 4–6

125g (4½oz) butter,
softened

4 garlic cloves,
finely grated

1 tbsp freshly
chopped parsley

8 sun-dried tomatoes,
snipped into pieces

1 ciabatta loaf, sliced
in half horizontally
(approximately
275g/10oz)

Mary's Tips

*Prepare up to 12 hours
ahead and cook to serve.*

Freezes well uncooked.

1. Preheat the grill to medium–high.

2. Measure the butter into a bowl and season with sea salt and
   freshly ground black pepper. Stir in the garlic, parsley and
   sun-dried tomato pieces.

3. Lay the pieces of ciabatta cut side up on a baking sheet and
   spread with the flavoured butter. Slide the baking sheet under
   the grill and cook the ciabatta for about 4 minutes or until
   golden and crisp.

4. Slice into pieces to serve.

Smoked Trout and Egg Mayo Tumbler

Easy to make as a first course, light lunch or supper. Presented in a tumbler, it is easy to eat just with a fork. The trout in this recipe is cold-smoked, like smoked salmon.

Serves 4

———

4 eggs

200g (7oz) smoked trout slices

4 tbsp full-fat mayonnaise

4 tbsp full-fat crème fraîche

4 spring onions, finely sliced

2 Little Gem lettuces

2 tomatoes, deseeded and diced

1 punnet mustard cress

Juice of ½ lemon

You will need 4 glass tumblers.

Mary's Tips

———

Can be assembled up to 4 hours ahead.

Not suitable for freezing.

1. Place the eggs in a saucepan of cold water. Bring up to the boil, then continue to boil for 8 minutes until hard boiled. Drain and run under cold water. When cool enough to handle, peel and chop into small dice.

2. Reserve four small slices of trout and finely chop the remainder.

3. Mix the mayonnaise, crème fraîche and spring onions in a bowl. Add the egg and chopped trout and lots of salt and freshly ground black pepper.

4. Reserve 4 of the Little Gem leaves and finely shred the remainder.

5. To assemble, place the shredded lettuce in the base of the tumblers. Spoon the egg and trout mixture on top, then add the tomatoes. Arrange a pile of cress next to the tomatoes and insert the reserved lettuce leaves into the side of the tumblers. Swirl the reserved trout slices and sit them on top. Finally, season with a little more black pepper and a squeeze of lemon juice.

Sticky Chicken Bites

**These will be loved by everyone. The sauce works
well with mini sausages, too.**

Serves 4–6

2 tbsp hoisin sauce

2 tbsp mango chutney

5cm (2in) fresh root
ginger, peeled
and grated

2 tsp tomato purée

1 tsp cornflour

2 large chicken
breasts, cut into
2cm (¾in) cubes

Mary's Tips

*Can be made up to
8 hours ahead and
warmed to serve.*

*Freezes well marinated
and raw.*

1. Mix the hoisin, mango chutney, ginger, tomato purée and
   cornflour together in a bowl.

2. Season the chicken cubes with salt and freshly ground
   black pepper and add to the marinade.

3. Preheat the grill to high and line a baking sheet with foil.

4. Arrange the chicken on the prepared baking sheet and
   slide under the grill for about 5–7 minutes, turning
   occasionally, until cooked through.

5. Arrange on a serving platter with cocktail sticks and
   serve warm.

Chicory and Beetroot Eats

**These are healthy and refreshing and make great nibbles for
a party or are lovely as part of a sharing platter.**

2 chicory heads
(red or white)

175g (6oz) cooked
beetroot, finely
diced (to the size
of a raisin)

2 tsp balsamic glaze

1 tsp soy sauce

1 tbsp olive oil

125g (4½oz) feta
cheese, crumbled

25g (1oz) pomegranate
seeds

½ small bunch of
coriander, leaves
finely chopped

Mary's Tips

*Can be assembled up
to 4 hours ahead.*

Not suitable for freezing.

1. Separate the large leaves from the chicory and arrange them on a serving platter.

2. Place the diced beetroot in a bowl with the balsamic glaze, soy sauce, olive oil and lots of salt and freshly ground black pepper. Mix well.

3. Divide the beetroot between the chicory leaves and top each one with the crumbled feta, pomegranate seeds and coriander.

4. Chill until ready to serve.

Goat's Cheese, Asparagus and Fig Bruschetta

This is a popular first course or lunch in our house, or for supper as an outside dinner. Any time of day, in fact! This is fresh and looks so good too.

Serves 4

12 asparagus spears, woody ends removed

½ French stick baguette, cut on the diagonal into 4

2–3 tbsp olive oil

200g (7oz) soft spreadable goat's cheese

4 small figs, each cut into 6

1 tsp caster sugar or runny honey

Mary's Tips

Can be assembled up to 4 hours ahead and grilled to serve.

Not suitable for freezing.

1. Preheat the grill to medium–high.

2. Place the asparagus in a saucepan of boiling salted water and blanch for 2 minutes. Drain and refresh under cold water. Drain again and dry on kitchen paper.

3. Brush both sides of each piece of baguette with olive oil and season well with salt and freshly ground black pepper. Place the baguette slices under the grill and grill for about 2–3 minutes on each side until golden and crisp.

4. Leave to cool slightly, then spread goat's cheese on each slice. Arrange 3 asparagus tips in the centre of each slice and three pieces of fig on either side. Brush the asparagus with olive oil and season. Sprinkle a little caster sugar or drizzle a little honey on top of the figs. Place back under the grill for about 4–5 minutes, or until the fig has softened slightly and the asparagus is tinged brown.

5. Serve warm.

Fish

Seafood Salad with Pickled Veg 42

Panko Prawns with Mango Chilli Dipping Sauce 45

Prawn Fried Rice with Vegetables 46

Lemongrass Crab Cakes with Cucumber
and Radish Salsa 49

Risotto with Prawns, Watercress and Lemon 50

Kedgeree with Spinach and Herbs 52

Poached Halibut with Clam and
Crème Fraîche Sauce 55

Langoustine Paella 56

Lobster Tail Thermidor 59

Tuna Steaks with Greek Salad 60

Fish Cioppino 63

Three Fish and Potato Gratin 64

Sesame Miso Trout 66

Coriander Salmon with Lime 69

Mackerel with Garlic Black Pepper Noisette 70

Seafood Salad with Pickled Veg

A truly luxurious fish salad for sharing. If you can't buy fresh crabmeat, use tinned white crabmeat instead.

Serves 6

For the pickle

55g (2oz) caster sugar

75ml (2½fl oz) white wine vinegar

1 large banana shallot, thinly sliced

½ bulb fennel, thinly sliced

¼ cucumber, halved lengthways and thinly sliced

For the salad

4 eggs

4 Little Gem lettuces, shredded

75g (3oz) lamb's lettuce

200g (7oz) fresh white crabmeat

300g (10½oz) cooked king prawns

150g (5oz) hot-smoked salmon fillets, flaked

115g (4oz) smoked salmon, cut into small pieces

For the dressing

Juice of ½ lemon

2 tbsp sun-dried tomato paste

8 tbsp olive oil

1. To make the pickle, measure the caster sugar and vinegar into a small saucepan. Stir over a medium heat until dissolved, then boil for 1 minute. Remove from the heat and add the shallot, fennel and cucumber. Season with salt and set aside for a minimum of 15–30 minutes, while the pickle cools.

2. Place the eggs in a saucepan, cover with water and bring to the boil. Boil for 5 minutes, then drain, cool, peel and slice into wedges.

3. Scatter the lettuces onto a very large flat platter. Add the crab in piles, then the prawns, hot-smoked salmon, smoked salmon and eggs.

4. Strain the pickle into a bowl (reserving the liquid), then spoon the pickle on top of the seafood.

5. Add the dressing ingredients to the reserved pickling liquid and whisk until smooth.

6. Season the dish with a little salt and freshly ground black pepper and drizzle with dressing just before serving.

Mary's Tips

Can be assembled up to 6 hours ahead. Dress just before serving.

Not suitable for freezing.

Panko Prawns
with Mango Chilli Dipping Sauce

Such a versatile dish. You can serve it as a main course with a side salad, as a starter or even as a nibble to go with drinks. It is essential to devein the prawns before cooking them.

600g (1lb 5oz) raw
  shell-on jumbo
  king prawns
55g (2oz) plain flour
125g (4½oz) fine
  panko breadcrumbs
2 eggs
Sunflower oil,
  for frying

For the marinade

1 tsp sunflower oil
1 garlic clove,
  finely grated
1 tsp finely grated
  fresh root ginger

For the dipping sauce

6 tbsp mango chutney
1 tsp finely grated
  fresh root ginger
Juice of 1 lemon
2 tsp soy sauce
½ red chilli, deseeded
  and diced

Mary's Tips

*Best prepared and
made to serve.*

Not suitable for freezing.

1. Remove the heads and shells from the prawns leaving the tail on. Devein the prawns and place them in a bowl. Add the marinade ingredients and mix well. Leave to marinate in the fridge for 30 minutes or longer.

2. Meanwhile, mix the dipping sauce ingredients together in a bowl.

3. Measure the flour onto a plate and season well with salt and freshly ground black pepper. Tip the panko breadcrumbs onto a separate plate. Break the eggs into a bowl and beat with a fork. Coat the prawns in the flour, then dip into the beaten egg and finally cover in the panko breadcrumbs.

4. Pour a layer of sunflower oil in a large deep frying pan, enough to cover the base of the pan, and place over a high heat. When hot, add the prawns and fry for 2 minutes (you will need to do this in batches). Turn the prawns over and fry on the second side for 2–3 minutes, until cooked through and golden. Remove from the pan and drain on kitchen paper to remove the excess oil.

5. Pile the prawns on to a serving plate and serve with the dipping sauce in a bowl alongside.

Prawn Fried Rice with Vegetables

A hearty bowl of goodness. Once you have the ingredients prepared, it is very quick to make. I think the packets of cooked rice are excellent for when you are short of time and they have no added ingredients.

Large knob of butter

350g (12oz) raw
  peeled tiger prawns

1 tbsp sunflower oil

1 large onion,
  roughly chopped

1 red pepper, deseeded
  and chopped

250g (9oz) chestnut
  button mushrooms,
  sliced

2 large garlic cloves,
  finely grated

150g (5oz) baby
  spinach

2 × 250g packets
  cooked basmati rice

1 tbsp hoisin sauce

1 tbsp sweet chilli sauce

2 tbsp soy sauce

Juice of ½ lemon

2 tsp sesame oil

Mary's Tips

Best prepared and made to serve.

Not suitable for freezing.

1. Place a large frying pan or wok over a high heat until hot. Add half the butter. When foaming, add the prawns, season with salt and freshly ground black pepper and fry for a few minutes, until pink. Transfer to a plate.

2. Add the sunflower oil and remaining butter to the unwashed pan. Stir in the onion and pepper and fry for about 3 minutes. Add the mushrooms and fry for 5 minutes, until most of the liquid has evaporated. Add the garlic and spinach and fry until wilted. Finally, stir in the rice and fry for 2–3 minutes until heated through.

3. Add the hoisin, sweet chilli and soy sauces, the lemon juice and sesame oil. Stir well.

4. Return the prawns to the pan and toss everything together.

5. Serve in hot bowls with chopsticks or a fork.

Lemongrass Crab Cakes
with Cucumber and Radish Salsa

This mixture can be made into 8 patties, if you are serving them for lunch or supper, or turned into tiny popcorn crab cakes for a canapé. Once the jar of lemongrass paste is open, it will keep in the fridge for 3 weeks or can be frozen for up to 3 months. If no lemongrass paste is available, use the grated zest of 1 lemon.

Makes 8 large or about 40 small cakes

———

450g (1lb) fresh
   white crabmeat
150g (5oz) panko
   breadcrumbs
2 tsp lemongrass
   paste from a jar
2 tsp grated fresh root ginger
4 tbsp full-fat mayonnaise
2 tbsp sweet chilli sauce
1 egg, beaten
1 small bunch of coriander,
   leaves roughly chopped
Sunflower oil, for frying

For the salsa

2 tbsp sweet chilli sauce
About 3 tbsp sunflower oil
1 tsp grated fresh root ginger
½ tsp lemongrass
   paste from a jar
½ large cucumber, peeled,
   deseeded and diced
6 radishes, thinly sliced
   into rounds
1 small bunch of coriander,
   leaves roughly chopped
4 spring onions,
   trimmed and sliced

1. To make the crab cakes, first check the crabmeat for any shell. Place the crabmeat in a bowl with 100g (3¾oz) of the breadcrumbs and lots of salt and freshly ground black pepper. Add the lemongrass paste, ginger, mayonnaise, sweet chilli sauce, egg and coriander. Mix well and shape into 8 large or about 40 tiny cakes.

2. Crush the remaining breadcrumbs to make a finer crumb, then coat the cakes to give a thin but even crust. Chill in the fridge until needed.

3. Meanwhile, mix all the salsa ingredients together in a bowl and season to taste.

4. When ready to serve, heat a little sunflower oil in a large frying pan over a medium heat. Fry the cakes in batches for about 2 minutes on each side until golden. Remove from the pan and set aside on kitchen paper to drain the excess oil.

5. Place on a large plate and serve with the salsa on the side.

Mary's Tips

———

Crab cakes can be made but not fried up to a day ahead.

Uncooked crab cakes freeze well.

Risotto with Prawns, Watercress and Lemon

Fresh and light, this is a great dish to serve to friends. Watercress is one of my favourite greens. It's underrated but I love it. It has a peppery flavour, so go easy when seasoning with pepper.

Serves 6

2 tbsp sunflower oil

40g (1½oz) butter

4 large banana shallots, sliced

1 large garlic clove, finely grated

300g (10½oz) risotto rice

1 litre (1¾ pints) boiling vegetable or chicken stock

175g (6oz) fresh watercress, coarsely chopped

75g (3oz) Parmesan, coarsely grated

115g (4oz) sour cream

Juice of 1 lemon

1 bunch of dill, finely chopped

350g (12oz) shelled raw prawns

Mary's Tips

Best made and served.

Not suitable for freezing.

1. Add the sunflower oil and a knob of the butter to a large frying pan over a high heat. Add the shallots and fry for a few minutes. Add the garlic and fry for 10 seconds. Add the rice and stir into the shallots.

2. Add ladles of hot stock to the rice, stirring the whole time, until all the liquid has been absorbed. This will take about 20 minutes.

3. Add the watercress, Parmesan, sour cream, lemon juice and dill. Gently stir until wilted. Season well with salt and some freshly ground black pepper.

4. Meanwhile, season the prawns and place a large frying pan over a high heat until hot. Add the remaining butter to the pan and, when it is foaming, add the prawns and quickly fry until they turn pink.

5. Add the prawns to the risotto just before serving.

Kedgeree with Spinach and Herbs

One of my absolute favourite dishes. Check halfway through the cooking time and if it looks a little dry, add a bit more stock.

Serves 6

400g (14 oz) undyed smoked haddock, skin on

2 knobs of butter

1 lemon, halved

1 tbsp olive oil

2 onions, finely chopped

1 garlic clove, finely grated

2 tsp ground cumin

2 tsp ground coriander

1 tsp ground turmeric

300g (10½oz) basmati rice

600ml (1 pint) vegetable stock

2 bay leaves

4 eggs

75g (3oz) baby spinach, roughly chopped

4 tbsp pouring double cream

1 tbsp freshly chopped parsley

1 tbsp freshly chopped dill

Mary's Tips

Best made and eaten straight away.

Not suitable for freezing.

1. Preheat the oven to 200°C/180°C fan/Gas 6. Line a baking tray with foil.

2. Place the haddock, skin-side down, on the prepared tray and put the knobs of butter on top of the fish. Cut one half of the lemon into 6 thin slices and lay them over the fish. Squeeze the remaining half over the fish. Fold the sides of the foil over to make a parcel, with the join at the side. Bake in the preheated oven for about 15–18 minutes, or until the fish is cooked and flakes easily. Peel off and remove the skin and set the fish aside.

3. Pour the oil into a large deep frying pan with a lid over a high heat. Add the onions and fry for 2–4 minutes. Add the garlic, spices and rice and stir to coat in the mixture. Pour in the stock and add the bay leaves. Season with salt and freshly ground black pepper, cover with a lid and bring up to the boil. Boil for 2 minutes, then reduce the heat and simmer very gently for about 12–15 minutes, until all the liquid has been absorbed and the rice is just cooked, but still with a slight bite.

4. Meanwhile, soft boil the eggs in boiling water for about 6 minutes. Peel and cut them into quarters. Set aside.

5. Stir the spinach into the rice until wilted. Add the cream and all the lemony, buttery fish juices from the haddock and mix together. Break the haddock into large pieces and scatter over the rice. Check the seasoning and spoon into a warmed serving dish.

6. Garnish with the fresh herbs and top with the soft-boiled eggs to serve.

Poached Halibut with Clam and Crème Fraîche Sauce

Halibut is a firm, flavourful white fish – a luxury, like turbot. A less expensive option would be seabass or cod, which would also work well with the clam sauce. Each halibut fillet serves 2 people. Treat clams the same as mussels – if they are open before cooking, throw them away; if they are closed after cooking, throw them away.

Serves 4

2 tbsp olive oil

Knob of butter

4 large banana shallots, finely chopped

2 garlic cloves, finely grated

75ml (2½fl oz) apple juice or white wine

2 × 175–200g (6–7oz) long halibut fillets, skin on

500g (1lb 2oz) fresh clams in their shells, cleaned and scrubbed

Juice of ½ lemon

200g (7oz) full-fat crème fraîche

3 tbsp freshly chopped parsley

300g (10½oz) French green beans

½ lemon, cut into wedges

Mary's Tips

Best made and served.

Not suitable for freezing.

1. Heat the oil and butter in a deep frying pan with a lid over a high heat. Add the shallots and fry for 3–4 minutes. Add the garlic and fry for 30 seconds. Pour in the apple juice or wine and bring up to the boil.

2. Season the halibut fillets with salt and freshly ground black pepper and place them skin-side down in the pan. Cover with a lid and gently poach over a low heat for about 8 minutes until the fish is soft to touch and just cooked. Carefully remove the fish from the pan and place on a warm plate. Cover and set aside to rest while finishing the sauce.

3. Add the clams to the pan, bring back up to the boil with the lid on for 1 minute, then stir in the lemon juice and crème fraîche. Return to the boil and simmer for 1 minute. Check the seasoning and stir in most of the parsley.

4. Meanwhile, cook the green beans in boiling salted water for 4 minutes. Drain well.

5. Divide the sauce between four bowls or plates. Arrange the beans on one side.

6. Carefully remove the skin from the fish and separate each fillet into two pieces. Place one piece of halibut on top of the clams in each bowl or plate.

7. Sprinkle with the remaining parsley and serve with a lemon wedge.

Langoustine Paella

An all-in-one pan, this is a real crowd pleaser and is full of vibrant colours and flavours. If you are unable to get langoustines, use large prawns. Saffron comes in little pots and is a very precious spice; it makes a paella what it is.

Serves 6–8

6 raw langoustines

2 tbsp olive oil

1 large onion, finely chopped

1 red pepper, deseeded and diced

4 garlic cloves, finely chopped

A good pinch of saffron

1 tbsp paprika

275g (10oz) paella or basmati rice

150ml (¼ pint) white wine

1 × 400g tin chopped tomatoes

600ml (1 pint) fish stock

250g (9oz) cod, skinned and sliced into large chunks

200g (7oz) squid, sliced

350g (12oz) mussels

55g (2oz) frozen petits pois

2 tbsp freshly chopped parsley, to serve (optional)

Lemon wedges, to serve

Mary's Tips

Best made and served.

Not suitable for freezing.

1. Bring a pan of salted water up to the boil. Add the langoustines and boil for 4–5 minutes until pink and cooked through. Drain and set aside.

2. Heat the oil in a large non-stick frying or two-handled paella pan over a high heat. Add the onion and fry for a few seconds. Add the pepper and fry for 4–5 minutes. Add the garlic and fry for 10 seconds.

3. Soak the saffron in 3 tablespoons of water.

4. Sprinkle the paprika and rice into the pan and stir to coat. Pour in the wine and add the saffron with its soaking liquid. Reduce the liquid over a high heat for a few seconds, stirring.

5. Add the chopped tomatoes and stock, stir and bring up to the boil. Reduce the heat and simmer gently uncovered for about 20 minutes, stirring occasionally, until almost all of the liquid has been absorbed. (You may need a little more stock, if it is too thick.)

6. Add the cod, squid and mussels to the pan, cover with a lid or tightly with foil and continue to cook for about 10 minutes until the cod, seafood and rice are cooked through and all the liquid has been absorbed. Stir in the peas for the last 5 minutes.

7. Place the cooked langoustines on top and serve sprinkled with chopped parsley, if using, and with lemon wedges alongside.

Lobster Tail Thermidor

Lobster tails are readily available to buy, and this is a real treat of a dish. It's easy to make ahead for a special supper. There are many different ways to cook and prepare lobster tails, but this is my preferred, foolproof way.

Serves 2

2 raw lobster tails, fresh or frozen

55g (2oz) lamb's lettuce, to serve

2 lemon wedges

For the sauce
Large knob of butter

1 banana shallot, finely chopped

75ml (2½fl oz) white wine

75ml (2½fl oz) fish stock

75ml (2½fl oz) pouring double cream

1 level tsp Dijon mustard

1 tbsp freshly chopped chives

1 tbsp freshly chopped parsley

20g (¾oz) Parmesan, finely grated

Mary's Tips

Can be prepared up to 6 hours ahead.

Not suitable for freezing.

1. To cook the lobster, thaw the tails, if frozen. Fill a pan with water, add a tablespoon of salt and bring to the boil. Once boiling, add the tails, cover with a lid, reduce the heat to a simmer and cook for about 7 minutes, until the tails have turned pink. Drain and rinse the tails in cold water. To remove the meat from the shell, place the tail on a board, rounded shell side down. Using sharp scissors, cut around the edge of the shell, remove and discard the skin surface, and scoop out the flesh. Cut the meat into bite-sized pieces, sprinkle with a little salt and pepper and set aside. Keep the shell.

2. To make the sauce, melt the butter in a saucepan over a high heat. Add the shallot and fry for a few minutes. Add the white wine and stock and reduce over the high heat by half. Pour in the cream and reduce by half again. Remove the pan from the heat and add the mustard, chives, parsley and season with salt and freshly ground black pepper. Stir the lobster pieces into the sauce.

3. Preheat the grill to medium–high.

4. Spoon the lobster and sauce back into the shells and sprinkle the top of each with the Parmesan. Place on a tray under the grill (not too near the top) and cook for about 8–10 minutes until golden and bubbling.

5. Serve arranged on two plates on a bed of lamb's lettuce with a wedge of lemon on the side.

Tuna Steaks with Greek Salad

Pan-fried tuna steaks with a light and healthy Greek salad – close your eyes and you could be on a Greek island! Be careful not to marinate the tuna steaks for too long, as they begin to 'cook' in the acidic juices.

4 tuna steaks

2 tbsp olive oil

Juice of ½ lemon

1 small garlic clove, finely grated

For the Greek salad

6 tbsp olive oil

Juice of ½ lemon

1 tbsp white wine vinegar

½ garlic clove, finely grated

2 tbsp coarsely chopped mint leaves

2 tbsp coarsely chopped coriander leaves

200g (7oz) cherry tomatoes, halved

½ cucumber, peeled, deseeded and diced

115g (4oz) small pitted black olives

200g (7oz) feta cheese, broken into pieces

Mary's Tips

Salad can be made 1 hour ahead.

Not suitable for freezing.

1. To marinate the tuna steaks, place the olive oil, lemon juice and garlic in a shallow dish and mix well. Add the tuna and coat in the mixture. Leave to marinate for 10 minutes but no longer.

2. Meanwhile, make the salad. Measure the olive oil, lemon juice, white wine vinegar and garlic into a large mixing bowl. Season with freshly ground black pepper and a little salt and mix together. Add the fresh herbs, cherry tomatoes, cucumber, olives and feta cheese. Stir carefully until coated in the dressing.

3. Place a large frying pan over a high heat until very hot. Season the tuna steaks, then add to the pan and fry for 1–1½ minutes on each side until browned, but still pink in the middle.

4. Divide the salad between four plates and top with a tuna steak. Spoon any leftover dressing over the tuna to serve.

Fish Cioppino

A hearty and healthy, Italian-style rustic fish stew with herbs and a variety of seafood. It originated in San Francisco and had been brought over to America by Italian immigrant fishermen who settled there. This is not unlike the French classic bouillabaisse, which has saffron in the tomato base. Serve with chunky bread or toasted sourdough.

Serves 6

2 tbsp olive oil

2 large onions, finely chopped

3 sticks celery, finely chopped

1 red pepper, deseeded and finely chopped

3 garlic cloves, finely grated

½ red chilli, deseeded and finely chopped

150ml (¼ pint) white wine

1 × 400g tin chopped tomatoes

2 tbsp tomato purée

300ml (½ pint) vegetable or fish stock

1 tbsp freshly chopped oregano

2 tsp freshly chopped thyme

250g (9oz) cod fillet, skinned and cut into 2cm (¾in) cubes

175g (6oz) raw shelled tiger prawns

250g (9oz) mussels, cleaned

2 tbsp freshly chopped parsley

1. Heat the oil in a large, deep, wide-based frying pan over a high heat. Add the onions, celery and pepper and fry for about 8 minutes until nearly soft. Add the garlic and chilli and fry for 30 seconds. Pour in the white wine and boil to evaporate by half.

2. Add the chopped tomatoes, purée, stock, oregano and thyme and return to the boil. Cover, reduce the heat and simmer for about 10–15 minutes, until the liquid has slightly reduced. Season well with salt and freshly ground black pepper.

3. Add the cod, prawns and mussels, cover and simmer for about 5 minutes, until the cod is cooked through, the prawns are pink and the mussels have opened.

4. Sprinkle with the parsley and check the seasoning. Serve with toasted sourdough and eat with a spoon and fork.

Mary's Tips

The tomato base can be made up to 8 hours ahead. Bring to the boil and add fish to serve.

The tomato base freezes well.

Three Fish and Potato Gratin

**A complete meal all in one dish. Perfect to make ahead. Many fishmongers
and good supermarkets sell packs of mixed and ready-prepared fish.**

Serves 6

4 eggs
350g (12oz) small new
  potatoes, halved
2 onions, roughly
  chopped
75g (3oz) butter
75g (3oz) plain flour
900ml (1½ pints)
  hot milk
125g (4½oz)
  mature Cheddar,
  coarsely grated
Juice of 1 large lemon
6 tbsp freshly
  chopped parsley
2 heaped tsp Dijon
  mustard
Grating of nutmeg
250g (9oz) baby spinach
500g (1lb 2oz) mixed fish
  (e.g. smoked haddock,
  salmon and cod), cut
  into 3cm (1¼in) cubes
115g (4oz) panko
  breadcrumbs or fresh
  white breadcrumbs

Mary's Tips

*Can be made up to 6 hours
ahead. Add the topping
just before baking.*

Not suitable for freezing.

1. Preheat the oven to 200°C/180°C Fan/Gas 6. You will need a 1.75-litre (3-pint) round or rectangle ovenproof dish.

2. Place the eggs in a saucepan, cover with water and bring to the boil. Boil for 8 minutes, then drain, cool, peel and slice into quarters.

3. Meanwhile, place the potatoes in a pan of salted water and bring up to the boil. Boil for 5 minutes, then add the onions to the pan and continue to boil for another 5 minutes, until the potatoes are tender. Drain and set aside.

4. To make the sauce, melt the butter in a wide saucepan over a medium heat. Sprinkle in the flour and stir over the heat for 10 seconds. Whisk in the hot milk, whisking until smooth and thickened. Add 50g of the cheese, the lemon juice, 4 tablespoons of the parsley, the mustard and nutmeg. Season well with salt and freshly ground black pepper.

5. Put the spinach into a colander. Pour over a kettle of boiling water to wilt the leaves. Run the spinach under cold water to refresh, then drain and squeeze out the liquid. Spread the spinach over the base of the ovenproof dish.

6. Add the potatoes, onions, quartered eggs and fish to the sauce and mix well. Spoon the fish mixture on top of the spinach.

7. Mix the breadcrumbs with the remaining cheese and parsley, then sprinkle over the top. Bake in the preheated oven for about 40–45 minutes until golden and bubbling around the edges.

8. Serve piping hot with a green vegetable or salad.

Sesame Miso Trout

A super-quick recipe. You'll just have to buy the fish; all the rest should be in the fridge or store cupboard. Buy fillets that are the same size and shape so they cook at the same rate. You could replace the pak choi with fresh spinach, if preferred.

Serves 4
———

4 × 125g (4½oz)
    raw fresh trout
    fillets, skin on
4 level tsp white
    miso paste
3 tbsp toasted
    sesame seeds
2 tbsp olive oil, plus a
    bit extra for the veg
Knob of butter
4 pak choi, sliced
    into large pieces
6 spring onions,
    finely sliced

For the glaze
4 tbsp sweet chilli sauce
1 tsp white miso paste
2 tsp olive or sesame oil

Mary's Tips
———

*Glaze can be made
ahead. Cook trout
and veg to serve.*

Not suitable for freezing.

1. Preheat the oven to 200°C/180°C Fan/Gas 6. Line a baking sheet with non-stick baking paper.

2. Whisk the glaze ingredients and 6 tablespoons of water together in a small bowl. Set aside.

3. Season the trout fillets with salt and freshly ground black pepper and spread the miso paste on the flesh side. Sprinkle the sesame seeds over the top of the miso and press down to stick the seeds to the paste.

4. Place the oil in a frying pan over a medium heat. Add the trout fillets, seeded side down, and fry for about 2–3 minutes, until golden brown. Very carefully turn the fillets over and fry for about 2 minutes on the skin side. Add the butter and, when foaming, use a teaspoon to coat the trout.

5. Transfer the fillets to the prepared baking sheet, skin-side down, and cook in the preheated oven for about 7–8 minutes, until just cooked through.

6. Meanwhile, wipe the pan clean, add a little oil and place over a high heat. Add the pak choi, spring onions and seasoning, and stir until just wilted.

7. Spoon on to a serving dish and place the trout fillets on top.

8. Add the glaze ingredients to the pan and gently warm until just bubbling. Spoon over the trout and serve at once.

Coriander Salmon with Lime

A quick and easy salmon recipe. The filling is delicious with trout fillets, too.

Serves 4
___

4 salmon fillets, skin on

1 small lime, halved
and thinly sliced

For the topping

165g (5¼oz) full-fat
cream cheese

1 egg yolk

2 tsp green or red
Thai curry paste

Finely grated zest
of ½ lime

2 tbsp freshly chopped
coriander

2 tsp sweet chilli sauce

Mary's Tips
___

*Can be prepared up
to 6 hours ahead.*

Not suitable for freezing.

1. Preheat the oven to 200°C/180°C Fan/Gas 6. Line a baking sheet with non-stick baking paper.

2. Mix the cream cheese, egg yolk, Thai curry paste, lime zest, coriander and sweet chilli sauce in a small bowl. Season well with salt and freshly ground black pepper.

3. Lift the salmon fillets onto a board skin-side down. Using a small, sharp knife, cut vertically down into the fillets, then continue this cut through the fillet leaving the top and bottom attached. Open the salmon out slightly to make a pocket in the flesh, season lightly.

4. Divide the topping between the fillets and arrange three thin slices of lime on top of each one. Lift the salmon fillets onto the prepared baking sheet and cook in the preheated oven for about 12–15 minutes until just cooked. The salmon should be opaque pink.

Mackerel with Garlic Black Pepper Noisette

Mackerel is a very rich oily fish that is deep in flavour. This sauce complements the fish particularly well.

Serves 4

4 fresh mackerel
  fillets, skin on
2 tbsp plain flour
1 tbsp sunflower oil
75g (3oz) butter
2 small garlic cloves,
  finely grated
Lemon wedges,
  to serve

Mary's Tips

Best made and served.

Not suitable for freezing.

1. Place the fillets on a board, skin-side down. Season well with salt and lots of freshly ground black pepper. Lightly dust the top with plain flour and press onto the mackerel.

2. Heat the oil in a large frying pan over a high heat. Add the fillets, skin-side down, and fry for 1 minute, then turn over and fry for about 2–3 minutes on the other side, until just cooked. Remove the fish from the pan and set aside on warm plates.

3. Add the butter to the pan and heat until a nutty brown colour. Add the garlic and remove from the heat. Swirl the garlic in the foaming butter then quickly pour over the fish.

4. Serve with lemon wedges.

Chicken

Chicken Chow Mein 76

Marinated Spiced Chicken with Herby Couscous 78

Pan-fried Ginger and Chilli Chicken
with Water Chestnuts 81

Red Roaring Chicken 83

Super Easy Mango Chicken 84

Garlic Chicken Fricassee 87

Honey Mustard Chicken with Rustic Potatoes 88

Amalfi Orzo Chicken 90

Sriracha Chicken Wings with Sriracha
and Sour Cream Dip 93

Coq au Vin Pie 95

Chicken Chow Mein

A gently spiced Chinese classic of stir-fried noodles, vegetables and chicken. Add the bean sprouts right at the end, just to heat through, or they will become too soft and make the noodles soggy. If you prefer beef chow mein, use 350g (12oz) trimmed and thinly sliced rump steak, and pan fry the strips for 2 minutes.

Serves 4

180g (6¼oz) fine
   egg noodles
2 chicken breasts,
   skinned and sliced
   into thin strips
1 tbsp runny honey
2 tbsp sunflower
   or sesame oil
1 small onion,
   finely chopped
15g (½oz) piece of fresh
   root ginger, peeled
   and finely grated
175g (6oz) chestnut
   button mushrooms,
   thickly sliced
2 garlic cloves,
   finely grated

For the sauce
2 tbsp black bean sauce
4 tbsp soy sauce
1 tbsp rice wine vinegar
   or white wine vinegar
1 tsp runny honey
2 spring onions, sliced
175g (6oz) bean sprouts

Mary's Tips

Cook to serve.

Not suitable for freezing.

1. Cook the noodles according to the packet instructions. Drain and set aside.

2. Toss the chicken in the runny honey. Meanwhile, heat half the oil in a large non-stick frying pan or wok and stir-fry the chicken over a high heat for a few minutes until browned. Remove from the pan and set aside.

3. Add the remaining oil to the pan, then the onion and cook over a high heat, covered with a lid, for about 2–3 minutes. Add a drop of water to prevent burning, if needed. Stir in the ginger, mushrooms and garlic, and fry for about 3 minutes until they start to soften.

4. Meanwhile, mix the black bean sauce, soy sauce, rice or white wine vinegar and honey together in a small bowl with 2 tablespoons of water.

5. Add the drained noodles to the pan with the vegetables, toss well, then add the sauces, spring onions and the cooked chicken. Stir-fry for a few minutes until piping hot.

6. Add the bean sprouts at the very last moment, season with plenty of black pepper and serve at once.

Marinated Spiced Chicken with Herby Couscous

This is a lovely complete dish with a sauce and a herby couscous salad. I sometimes serve it with a tomato salad alongside, too.

Serves 4

3 large chicken breasts, skinned and cut into 2cm (¾in) slices

2 tbsp runny honey

For the marinade

200g (7oz) full-fat natural yoghurt

1 small garlic clove, finely grated

1 tbsp grated fresh root ginger

Zest and juice of ½ lemon

1 tsp ground cumin

For the couscous salad

150g (5oz) couscous

200ml (⅓ pint) hot chicken stock

2 tbsp olive oil

1 bunch of mint, leaves chopped

1 bunch of coriander, leaves chopped

¼ cucumber, peeled into ribbons

For the herb sauce

250g (9oz) full-fat natural yoghurt

Juice of ½ lemon

2 tsp mint sauce, from a jar

1. To make the marinade, measure all the ingredients into a bowl and mix well. Add the chicken pieces, toss until coated and leave to marinate in the fridge for 1 hour.

2. Meanwhile, to make the salad, place the couscous and hot stock in a bowl. Cover with cling film and leave for about 15 minutes until the couscous has absorbed all the liquid. Once dry and puffy, add the olive oil, half the herbs and season with salt and freshly ground black pepper. Stir to combine.

3. To make the sauce, measure the yoghurt, lemon juice, mint sauce and the remaining herbs into a bowl. Mix well and season.

4. Preheat the grill to high. Line a large baking sheet with foil.

5. Place the marinated chicken pieces on the prepared baking sheet, leaving space between each piece. Drizzle with the honey and season well. Place under the hot grill for about 6 minutes (this will depend on the thickness of the chicken slices), turning halfway, until tinged brown at the edges and cooked through.

6. Stir the cucumber ribbons into the couscous salad and divide between four plates. Arrange the chicken on top and serve with the herb sauce on the side.

Mary's Tips

Chicken can be marinated up to a day ahead. Sauce can be made up to two days ahead. Couscous can be made up to a day ahead. Add the cucumber before serving.

Not suitable for freezing.

Pan-fried Ginger and Chilli Chicken with Water Chestnuts

Chicken breasts with a ginger, garlic and mushroom sauce. There is an added surprise of water chestnuts, which give a lovely crunch.

Serves 6

6 small chicken breasts, skinned
2 tbsp sunflower oil
2 level tbsp cornflour
1 banana shallot, finely chopped
250g (9oz) small chestnut button mushrooms, halved
300ml (½ pint) chicken stock
4 tbsp full-fat crème fraîche
1 × 275g tin water chestnuts, thinly sliced if whole
2 tbsp freshly chopped coriander

For the marinade
1 tbsp runny honey
2 garlic cloves, finely grated
1 tsp finely grated fresh root ginger
1 red chilli, deseeded and fincly chopped
3 tbsp soy sauce
3 tbsp hoisin sauce

Mary's Tips

Can be made ahead on the day of serving.

Freezes well.

1. Slice the chicken breasts in half horizontally, to make 12 thin and flat fillets.

2. To make the marinade, measure the ingredients into a large bowl and mix together with a fork. Add the chicken breasts, toss to coat and marinate in the fridge for 1 hour.

3. Heat half the oil in a large frying pan over a high heat. Remove the chicken from the marinade (reserving the liquid marinade) and place in a single layer in the pan (you may need to do this in batches). Brown the chicken for about 3 minutes, turning halfway, until golden. Transfer the chicken to a plate and wipe the pan with damp kitchen paper to remove any dark marinade residue.

4. Mix the cornflour with 4 tablespoons of water in a small bowl until smooth.

5. Heat the remaining oil in the cleaned pan over a high heat. Add the shallot and mushrooms and fry for a few minutes. Add the reserved marinade, the stock and crème fraîche and bring to the boil, stirring continuously. Stir in the cornflour mixture, season with salt and freshly ground black pepper and bring to the boil to thicken.

6. Add the water chestnuts and return the chicken to the pan. Cover, reduce the heat and simmer gently for 5 minutes, until the chicken is cooked through and the sauce is coating the back of a spoon.

7. Arrange 2 thin fillets on each plate, sprinkle with the coriander and serve with rice.

Red Roaring Chicken

I like to do a recipe for a cold chicken salad in my books, to give the perfect prepare-ahead chicken dish for a large event. Serve this with green leaves and new potatoes, if liked.

Serves 6

200g (7oz) chargrilled
    red peppers from
    a jar, drained

150g (5oz) full-fat
    cream cheese

115g (4oz) full-fat
    crème fraîche

1 large bunch
    of basil, leaves
    roughly chopped

2 garlic cloves,
    finely grated

1 small bunch of
    chives, snipped

Zest and juice of
    ½ large lemon

3 tbsp mayonnaise

2 spring onions,
    finely sliced

750g (1lb 10oz) cooked
    chicken, cut into
    2cm (¾in) pieces

Mary's Tips

Can be made up to a day ahead. Sauce on its own can be kept in the fridge for up to 3 days.

Not suitable for freezing.

1. Slice half the peppers into cubes and set aside. Place the remaining peppers in a food processor with the cream cheese, crème fraîche, basil, garlic, chives and lemon zest and juice. Whiz until finely chopped and sauce consistency.

2. Spoon the sauce into a large bowl and add the mayonnaise and lots of salt and freshly ground black pepper. Mix well. Add the spring onions and chicken and stir to coat. Cover and chill in the fridge until needed.

3. To serve, spoon into a large serving dish and scatter with the reserved red peppers.

Super Easy Mango Chicken

This is one for midweek when you have no time at all. It's quick to make and cook in the oven. A simple dish but it tastes great, with a slightly curried aromatic flavour.

Serves 4–6

500g (1lb 2oz)
  boneless and skinless
  chicken thighs
2 tsp medium
  curry powder
2 tsp paprika
1 tsp garam masala
2 tbsp sunflower oil
2 onions, thinly sliced
200g (7oz) full-fat
  crème fraîche
2 tsp grated fresh
  root ginger
1 garlic clove,
  finely grated
Juice of ½ lemon
3 tbsp mango chutney
½ tsp ground turmeric
2 tbsp freshly chopped
  parsley (optional)

Mary's Tips

Can be made and assembled up to 12 hours ahead. Chill the covered dish and keep in the fridge for up to 12 hours. Cook to serve.

Not suitable for freezing.

1. Preheat the oven to 200°C/180°C Fan/Gas 6.

2. Season the chicken thighs with salt and freshly ground black pepper and sprinkle with 1 teaspoon each of the curry powder, paprika and garam masala.

3. Heat 1 tablespoon of the oil in a large frying pan over a high heat. Add the chicken and brown quickly on both sides. Remove from the pan and set aside in an ovenproof dish.

4. Add the remaining oil and the onions to the pan and fry over a high heat for a few minutes. Cover with a lid and cook for about 10 minutes until soft. Spoon the onion into the ovenproof dish with the chicken.

5. To make the sauce, measure the crème fraîche into a bowl. Mix in the ginger, garlic, lemon juice, mango chutney, turmeric and the remaining spices. Spoon over the chicken and onion, cover the dish with a lid or foil and cook in the preheated oven for about 25–30 minutes, until the chicken is cooked through.

6. Sprinkle with the parsley, if using, to serve.

Garlic Chicken Fricassee

This recipe is inspired by a traditional French dish. When I have time, I find this way of poaching chicken to be the best for tender pieces. If vermouth isn't available use dry white wine.

Serves 6–8

1 × 2kg (4lb 7oz)
  whole chicken

For the poaching liquid
750ml (1¼ pints)
  chicken stock
2 banana shallots, sliced
2 celery sticks, sliced
8 tsp black peppercorns
½ lemon
1 large bulb garlic, cut
  in half horizontally
  through the middle

For the sauce
Large knob of butter
500g (1lb 2oz) banana
  shallots, thinly sliced
3 sticks celery, finely diced
200ml (⅓ pint) vermouth
2 tbsp cornflour
200ml (⅓ pint) pouring
  double cream
3 tbsp freshly
  chopped chives
3 tbsp freshly
  chopped parsley

Mary's Tips

*Can be made up to
8 hours ahead.*

Freezes well.

1. Place the chicken in a large, wide-based, deep saucepan with a lid. Add all the poaching liquid ingredients and bring up to the boil. Cover with a lid, reduce the heat and simmer very gently for about 1 hour, until the chicken is just cooked. Remove from the heat and leave the chicken to cool in the pan.

2. Once cold, take out the chicken and remove the meat from the carcass. Slice the meat into large pieces and set aside. Strain the poaching liquid through a sieve into a large jug. Squeeze the garlic from their skins into a small bowl and mash with a fork. Discard the remaining poaching vegetables, lemon and peppercorns.

3. To make the sauce, melt the butter in a large frying pan over a medium heat. Add the shallots and celery and cook for about 8–10 minutes until soft. Add the mashed garlic and fry for 10 seconds. Pour in the vermouth and boil to reduce by half. Add 600ml (1 pint) of the strained poaching liquid, bring to the boil and boil rapidly for about 3 minutes.

4. Slake the cornflour with 2 tablespoons of the remaining cold poaching liquid in a cup. Stir this into the pan and cook until the sauce has thickened to a coating consistency. Add the cream and cooked chicken and reheat gently until hot through. Add the fresh herbs and season well with salt and freshly ground black pepper.

5. Serve with a green veg and mashed potatoes, rice or chunky bread.

Honey Mustard Chicken
with Rustic Potatoes

Great for a gang, especially if you have hungry teenagers. An all-in-one roasting tin – just serve with salad or a fresh slaw. You will need a large roasting tin, so the liquid evaporates and the potatoes can get crispy.

Serves 4–6

4 chicken legs

750g (1lb 10oz) new potatoes, halved or cut into three if big

2 tbsp olive oil

For the honey and mustard glaze

2 tbsp grainy mustard

3 tbsp tomato ketchup

1 tbsp Worcestershire sauce

1 garlic clove, finely grated

1 tbsp honey

Mary's Tips

Can be assembled up to an hour ahead.

Freezes well cooked.

1. Preheat the oven to 220°C/200°C Fan/Gas 7. Line a large shallow roasting tin with non-stick baking paper.

2. Mix all the glaze ingredients together in a small bowl.

3. Score the chicken legs, using a sharp knife, with three slashes across the skin, cutting into the meat a little bit. Sit the legs, skin-side up, on one side of the roasting tin. Spread the glaze over the chicken and season with salt and freshly ground black pepper.

4. Place the new potatoes and olive oil in a bowl. Add some seasoning and toss to coat the potatoes in the oil. Tip into the tin next to the chicken, so they do not overlap. Roast in the preheated oven for about 35–40 minutes, until the chicken is cooked through.

5. Place the chicken on a plate and cover with foil to rest. Gently turn the potatoes in the tin to coat in any leftover glaze and spread out in a single layer. Slide back into the oven for a further 8–10 minutes, until the potatoes are crispy and golden brown.

6. Serve the chicken and potatoes with the Lemon and Chive Coleslaw on page 178.

Amalfi Chicken Orzo

**A simple pasta dish with a creamy and delicious sauce. Orzo
are tiny pasta pearls that give a risotto-type dish.**

275g (10oz) orzo pasta
2 chicken breasts, skin
    removed and sliced
    into thin strips
2 tbsp runny honey
2 tbsp olive oil
Knob of butter
1 onion, finely chopped
250g (9oz)
    button chestnut
    mushrooms, sliced
150ml (¼ pint)
    white wine
1 garlic clove,
    finely grated
150g (5oz) baby
    spinach
150g (5oz) sour cream
55g (2oz) Parmesan,
    finely grated
1 tbsp fresh lemon juice

Mary's Tips

Best made and served.

Not suitable for freezing.

1. Cook the orzo in boiling salted water until just tender
   according to the packet instructions. Drain and set aside.

2. Season the chicken well with salt and freshly ground black
   pepper and toss in the runny honey. Heat the oil in a deep
   frying pan with a lid over a high heat. Add the chicken
   and fry for a few minutes, turning occasionally, until golden
   brown and just cooked. Remove the chicken from the pan
   and set aside.

3. Melt the butter in the same, unwashed pan. Add the
   onion and fry over a high heat for a few minutes, stirring
   occasionally, then cover and cook for 10 minutes until soft.

4. Remove the lid, add the mushrooms and fry until the liquid
   has evaporated from the mushrooms. Pour in the wine and
   reduce slightly. Add the garlic, spinach and sour cream
   and bring to the boil.

5. Finally add the orzo, cooked chicken, Parmesan and lemon
   juice to the pan. Check the seasoning and toss together until
   hot through.

6. Serve in bowls with a green salad.

Sriracha Chicken Wings
with Sriracha and Sour Cream Dip

One for when all the family get together. Teenagers with love these! Sriracha is a hot chilli sauce made with chillis, garlic and vinegar; different brands vary in density of heat and spice. It is best to buy complete chicken wings (not just the wing tips), which will have more meat on them.

1kg (2lb 4oz) large chicken wings, without tips (about 12)

2 tbsp sunflower oil, plus extra for drizzling

2 tsp sriracha sauce

15g (½oz) plain flour

1 tsp paprika

2 tsp ground ginger

For the sriracha dip

150g (5oz) sour cream

2 tbsp full-fat mayonnaise

Juice of ½ lemon

2 tsp sriracha sauce

2 tbsp freshly chopped chives, plus extra to garnish

Mary's Tips

Can be marinated up to 12 hours ahead. Dip can be made up to 2 days ahead.

Raw marinated wings freeze well.

1. Preheat the oven to 220°C/200°C Fan/Gas 7. Line a large roasting tin with non-stick baking paper.

2. Place the chicken wings in a bowl. Add the oil and sriracha sauce and season well with salt and freshly ground black pepper. Mix together well. Sprinkle the flour, paprika and ginger over the chicken and toss everything together.

3. Tip the wings into the prepared roasting tin and roast in the preheated oven for about 25 minutes. Remove from the oven and turn the wings over. Drizzle with a little oil and return to the oven for another 10–15 minutes, until the wings are golden and crisp.

4. Meanwhile, mix all the dip ingredients together in a small bowl and season well.

5. Pile the wings onto a serving plate and place the dip alongside. Garnish with extra chives to serve.

Coq au Vin Pie

A classic coq au vin but with a puff pastry topping. Why didn't we think of this before?! Poaching the chicken gives a wonderful tender chicken filling. If you are in a hurry, you could poach 5 chicken breasts instead of a whole chicken.

Serves 6–8

1 × 1.5kg (3lb 5oz) whole chicken

2 sticks celery, sliced

1 large onion, halved

2 carrots, sliced

2 bay leaves

2 chicken stock pots or cubes

1 × 500g block puff pastry

1 egg, beaten

For the filling

600ml (1 pint) red wine

2 tbsp olive oil

450g (1lb) shallots, peeled and left whole

200g (7oz) smoked streaky bacon, finely chopped

200g (7oz) button mushrooms

3 large garlic cloves, finely grated

2 tbsp tomato purée

4 tbsp brandy

50g (1¾oz) plain flour

600ml (1 pint) chicken stock

2 tbsp freshly chopped oregano

2 tsp Worcestershire sauce

Dash of gravy browning

Dash of sugar

1. You will need a 2-litre (3½-pint) ovenproof dish with a lip about 28cm (11in) diameter.

2. To poach the chicken, place the whole chicken in a tight-fitting deep saucepan with a lid. Add the celery, onion, carrots, bay leaves, stock pots or cubes and enough water to just cover the chicken. Bring up to the boil, then reduce the heat to a very low simmer, cover with a lid and simmer gently for about 1 hour, until the chicken is cooked through. Carefully remove the chicken to a dish and leave to cool.

3. Pour the wine into a saucepan and boil over a high heat for about 10 minutes to reduce by a third (to 300ml/½ pint). Set aside to cool.

4. Pour the oil into a large frying pan over a high heat. Add the shallots and bacon and fry for about 10 minutes, until the shallots are lightly golden and nearly soft. Add the mushrooms and fry for a few more minutes. Add the garlic and tomato purée and fry for 10 seconds.

5. Mix the brandy and flour together in a bowl. Whisk together to make a paste. Pour in the reduced cold wine and whisk until smooth. Add this liquid to the pan and boil and bubble for a few seconds. Pour in the stock and bring up to the boil, stirring until thickened. Add the oregano, Worcestershire sauce and season with salt and freshly ground black pepper. Simmer with the lid on for about 10 minutes. Add the gravy browning and sugar. Set aside.

Recipe continued

*Can be assembled up
to 6 hours ahead. The
filling can be made
up to a day ahead.*

*Freezes well with
raw pastry on top.*

6. Remove the chicken meat from the carcass and slice into bite-sized pieces. Add the meat to the sauce, stir to incorporate, then spoon into the pie dish. Set aside to cool.

7. Preheat the oven to 220°C/200°C Fan/Gas 7.

8. Roll out the pastry to be slightly bigger than the dish. Slice a long strip from the pastry and stick it to the lip of the dish using water. Brush the pastry on the lip with beaten egg, then lay the pastry on top. Press down to seal. Trim the edges and crimp. Brush the surface with the beaten egg. Roll out any trimmings and create stars with a cutter and arrange them in the centre of the pie. Brush with more beaten egg. Use a small sharp knife to make a hole to allow the steam to escape and prevent the pastry from being soggy.

9. Cook in the preheated oven for about 35–40 minutes, until well risen and golden on top and heated through in the middle. Serve with green vegetables.

Pork, Beef, Lamb
and Game

———

Parma Ham and Cauliflower Cheese Parcels

Serve them individually as a side dish or serve two per person and add some garlic bread as a main course. These are soooo good! It is important that the florets become cold when refreshed under cold water, so they do not continue to cook or become too soft.

Makes 6

300g (10½oz) cauliflower, broken into small florets (about the size of a strawberry)
150g (5oz) full-fat cream cheese
1 egg, beaten
75g (3oz) mature Cheddar, coarsely grated
25g (1oz) Parmesan, coarsely grated
1 tsp Dijon mustard
12 slices Parma ham

Mary's Tips

Parcels can be assembled up to 6 hours ahead.

Not suitable for freezing.

1. Preheat the oven to 220°C/200°C Fan/Gas 7. Line a large baking sheet with non-stick baking paper.

2. Bring a pan of salted water to the boil. Add the cauliflower and boil for about 3–4 minutes, until slightly soft, but still with bite. Drain and refresh under cold water. Drain again well.

3. Mix the cream cheese, egg, cheeses and mustard together in a large bowl. Season lightly with salt and freshly ground black pepper. Add the cooked cauliflower florets and carefully mix to coat the cauliflower but not to break the florets apart.

4. Put one slice of Parma ham on a board. Place a second slice on top to make a cross. Spoon a sixth of the mixture into the centre of the cross. Fold over the ham to encase the mixture. Repeat with the remaining slices.

5. Place the parcels on the prepared baking sheet and cook in the preheated oven for about 15–18 minutes until crispy.

6. Serve with a green salad.

Jacob's Spaghetti

Lucy's nephew loves this recipe. It is quick and easy for him and his mates at uni, and is a great recipe for the teenagers to make themselves.

Serves 4

300g (10½oz) spaghetti
1 tbsp olive oil
1 onion, finely chopped
115g (4oz) chorizo
  sausage, chopped
  into small pieces
1 garlic clove,
  finely grated
125g (4½oz) full-
  fat mascarpone
3 tbsp sun-dried
  tomato paste
275g (10oz) cherry
  tomatoes
150g (5oz) baby
  spinach

Mary's Tips

Best made and served.

Not suitable for freezing.

1. Cook the spaghetti according to the packet instructions until al dente. Drain and set aside.

2. Meanwhile, heat the oil in a wide frying pan over a high heat. Add the onion and chorizo and fry for a few minutes until golden brown. Add the garlic and fry for a minute.

3. Stir in the mascarpone and sun-dried tomato paste and season with salt and freshly ground black pepper. Add the cherry tomatoes and cook for 4 minutes, then add the baby spinach and cook for another 2 minutes, until the spinach has just wilted but is still bright green and holding its shape.

4. Stir in the spaghetti, coating in the sauce.

5. Tip into a hot serving bowl to serve.

Chimichurri Pork

Chimichurri is a wonderful, aromatic sauce from Latin America. It isn't cooked and will keep for up to a week in the fridge. It is delicious with this pork fillet but also works well stirred through pasta. The sauce can be made in a food processor, if liked, but keep it chunky. The flavours will infuse and become more pungent over time.

Serves 4

1 large pork fillet
(about 350g/12oz),
trimmed

For the marinade
2 tbsp olive oil
Juice of ½ lemon
2 garlic cloves,
finely grated
1 tsp paprika
1 tsp chilli flakes

For the chimichurri
3 tbsp finely chopped
fresh oregano
2 tbsp finely chopped
fresh coriander
1 tbsp freshly
chopped parsley
1 banana shallot,
finely chopped
Juice of ½ lemon
1 large garlic clove,
finely grated
½ tsp chilli flakes
8 tbsp olive oil

1. Put all the marinade ingredients into a large bowl, season with salt and freshly ground black pepper and mix well. Add the pork to the marinade and turn to coat. Leave to marinate for 1 hour, or longer if you have time.

2. Preheat the oven to 220°C/200°C Fan/Gas 7.

3. Place a frying pan over a high heat until hot. Add the pork fillet and fry until brown on all sides. Transfer to a small roasting tin and roast in the preheated oven for about 18 minutes, or until just cooked through. Cover with foil and set aside to rest.

4. Measure the sauce ingredients into a small jug or bowl. Season well and mix to combine.

5. Carve the pork into slices and serve with the sauce on the side.

Mary's Tips

Pork can be marinated up to a day ahead.

The raw pork can be frozen in the marinade.

Sausages with Mustard Mash
and Onion Gravy

A classic recipe but one with a delicious onion gravy. Choose your favourite flavoured sausage from your local butcher.

8 large pork sausages
600g (1lb 5oz) potatoes,
  peeled and cut into
  5cm (2in) cubes
  (prepared weight)
Large knob of butter
About 2 tbsp milk
2 tbsp grainy mustard

For the onion gravy
30g (1oz) butter
1 tbsp olive oil
1 large onion,
  thinly sliced
30g (1oz) plain flour
600ml (1 pint) hot
  beef stock
1 tsp Worcestershire
  sauce
1 tsp gravy browning
  (optional)

Mary's Tips

Onion gravy can be made up to 2 days ahead.

Gravy freezes well.

1. Preheat the oven to 200°C/180°C Fan/Gas 6. Line a roasting tin with non-stick baking paper.

2. Arrange the sausages in the prepared tin and roast in the preheated oven for about 30–40 minutes, turning halfway through, until cooked through. (You could also grill or fry the sausages.)

3. Meanwhile, place the potatoes in a pan of cold salted water. Cover with a lid and bring up to the boil. Boil for about 15 minutes, or until tender. Drain well, then tip the potatoes back into the pan and mash. Add the butter, milk and mustard and mix together well. Season with salt and freshly ground black pepper.

4. To make the gravy, melt the butter and oil in a saucepan over a medium heat. Add the onion and cook for about 5–8 minutes, until soft and tinged brown. Add the flour and stir for a few seconds. Blend in the stock gradually and bring up to the boil, stirring until thickened. Add the Worcestershire sauce and gravy browning, if using, and simmer for 4– 5 minutes. Check the seasoning.

5. Serve two sausages per person with some mash and gravy alongside.

Roast Rib of Beef
with Parsnips and Carrots

A wonderful family roast. I find it easier to carve if the rib of beef has been boned and rolled. If you have a particularly fatty piece of beef, you may need to strain off some of the fat from the vegetables after resting the meat and before returning the veg to the oven to crispen up.

Serves 6–8

1.7kg (3lb 12oz) boned and rolled rib of beef

4 tbsp sunflower oil

500g (1lb 2oz) medium parsnips, each sliced into 4 long, thin pieces

500g (1lb 2oz) medium carrots, each sliced into 3 long, thin pieces

5 bay leaves

For the gravy

40g (1½oz) butter

40g (1½oz) plain flour

600ml (1 pint) hot beef stock

150ml (¼ pint) red wine

1 tbsp Worcestershire sauce

A little gravy browning (optional)

Mary's Tips

Cold beef is delicious if there is some left over.

Not suitable for freezing.

1. Remove the beef from the fridge for 1 hour before roasting to come up to room temperature.

2. Preheat the oven to 220°C/200°C Fan/Gas 7.

3. Rub 2 tablespoons of oil over the beef and season well with salt and freshly ground black pepper.

4. Place the parsnips, carrots and bay leaves in a bowl, drizzle over the remaining oil and season well. Toss together, then tip into a medium roasting tin. Place a grill rack over the top of the vegetables and sit the beef on the rack. Roast in the preheated oven for about 1¼ hours, until dark golden and pink in the middle. Remove the beef to a board and cover with foil. Set aside to rest for about 30 minutes.

5. Meanwhile, slide the vegetables back into the oven if they need longer to crispen up.

6. To make the gravy, melt the butter in a saucepan over a medium heat. Add the flour and whisk for a few seconds. Whisk in the hot beef stock and wine and bring up to the boil. Cook until a smooth slightly thickened sauce consistency, then stir in the Worcestershire sauce, a dash of gravy browning, if using, and any juices from the beef.

7. Carve the beef into thin slices and serve with the vegetables and gravy. This goes well with the Hot Beetroot and Horseradish on page 193.

Cottage Pie with
Grated Double Potato Topping

A classic dish but we've added a two-potato topping.

Serves 6

2 tbsp sunflower oil
2 large onions, finely chopped
2 sticks celery, finely chopped
1 large carrot, finely chopped
1kg (2lb 4oz) lean beef mince
55g (2oz) plain flour
200ml (⅓ pint) Port
500ml (18fl oz) hot
  beef stock
1 tbsp sun-dried tomato paste
2 tbsp Worcestershire sauce
1 tbsp chopped fresh oregano
2 bay leaves
1 tsp gravy browning
  (optional)
500g (1lb 2oz) sweet potatoes
  (all a similar size)
750g (1lb 10oz) Maris Piper
  potatoes (all a similar size)
55g (2oz) butter, melted
55g (2oz) mature
  Cheddar, grated

Mary's Tips

*Can be made up to
8 hours ahead.*

*Freezes well without
the potato topping.*

1. Preheat the oven to 160°C/140°C Fan/Gas 3. You will need a round ovenproof dish about 28cm (11in) diameter.

2. Pour the oil into a large deep ovenproof frying pan with a lid over a high heat. Add the onions, celery and carrot and fry for a few minutes. Add the mince and brown over the heat with the vegetables.

3. Sprinkle in the flour and blend in the Port and stock. Stir until thickened slightly. Add the sun-dried tomato paste, Worcestershire sauce, marjoram or oregano and bay leaves. Cover with a lid and transfer to the oven for about 1–1½ hours, until the meat is tender.

4. Season well with salt and freshly ground black pepper, remove the bay leaves and stir in the gravy browning, if using. Spoon into the ovenproof dish and set aside.

5. Increase the oven temperature to 200°C/180°C Fan/Gas 6.

6. Meanwhile, place the potatoes in their skins in a large saucepan. Cover with salted water and bring to the boil. Boil for about 15–20 minutes until the potatoes are just cooked (they should still be firm to grate). Drain the potatoes and leave to cool in the colander until cold.

7. Peel the potatoes and coarsely grate using a box grater into a bowl. Add the melted butter and season. Spread over the cottage pie filling, then sprinkle with the cheese. Bake in the preheated oven for about 30–35 minutes, until golden brown and bubbling.

8. Serve hot with a green vegetable.

Penne Bolognaise Bake

Great for the family, bursting with flavour and we've used penne instead of lasagne sheets, so it is very easy to serve.

2 tbsp olive oil
500g (1lb 2oz)
  beef mince
1 large onion, chopped
2 garlic cloves,
  finely grated
2 × 400g tins chopped
  tomatoes
2 tbsp tomato purée
1 tsp caster sugar
Small bunch of basil,
  leaves chopped
200g (7oz) penne pasta

For the cheese sauce
55g (2oz) butter
55g (2oz) plain flour
600ml (1 pint) hot milk
2 tsp Dijon mustard
115g (4oz) mature
  Cheddar, grated
55g (2oz) Parmesan,
  grated

Mary's Tips

*Can be made up to
24 hours ahead.*

Freezes well.

1. Preheat the oven to 200°C/180°C Fan/Gas 6. Butter a large 23 × 28cm (9 × 11in) ovenproof dish.

2. Heat the oil in a large frying pan over a high heat. Add the beef and fry for few minutes until browned, breaking up with a wooden spoon as it fries. Add the onion and fry for about 5 minutes, then add the garlic and fry for 10 seconds. Stir in the tomatoes, tomato purée, sugar and basil, cover with a lid and simmer for 40 minutes over a low heat.

3. Meanwhile, cook the pasta according to the packet instructions. Drain and refresh with cold water. Drain again.

4. To make the cheese sauce, melt the butter in a saucepan over a medium heat. Add the flour and stir for a few seconds. Whisk in the milk and continue whisking until smooth and thickened. Add the mustard and Cheddar, and season well with salt and freshly ground black pepper.

5. Spoon the mince mixture into the base of the ovenproof dish. Tip the pasta on top and spread out evenly. Pour the cheese sauce over the pasta, then sprinkle with the Parmesan. Bake in the preheated oven for about 25–30 minutes until bubbling.

Highland Beef Pie

Perfect for feeding a gang, make this ahead and enjoy as a feast around Christmas time. If liked, you could replace 200g (7oz) beef with the same quantity of venison.

Serves 6–8

2 tbsp sunflower oil

1kg (2lb 4oz) beef shin, trimmed and cut into 5cm (2in) cubes

2 onions, thinly sliced

3 sticks celery, thinly sliced

2 garlic cloves, finely grated

55g (2oz) plain flour

500ml (18fl oz) red wine

300ml (½ pint) beef stock

1 tbsp tomato purée

1 tbsp freshly chopped thyme

1 × 390g jar pickled walnuts, drained and quartered

1 × 500g (1lb 2oz) block puff pastry

1 egg, beaten

Mary's Tips

Filling can be made up to a day ahead. Add the pastry top up to 4 hours ahead.

Freezes well.

1. Preheat the oven to 160°C/140°C Fan/Gas 3. You will need about a 1.75-litre (3-pint) round or rectangle ovenproof dish.

2. Heat the oil in a large casserole or a deep, ovenproof frying pan with a lid over a high heat. Add the beef and brown in batches until sealed. Remove from the pan and set aside.

3. Add the onions and celery to the pan and fry for about 4–5 minutes. Add the garlic and fry for 30 seconds. Return the beef to the pan.

4. Measure the flour into a mixing bowl. Whisk in the wine until smooth. Add the stock, wine mixture, purée and thyme to the pan, stirring to combine. Bring up to the boil. Cover with a lid and transfer to the oven for about 3–3½ hours.

5. Once the beef is tender, remove from the oven and stir in the pickled walnuts. Invert a small tea cup or pie funnel into the centre of the ovenproof dish, then spoon in the beef and leave to cool.

6. Increase the oven temperature to 200°C/180°C Fan/Gas 6.

7. Roll out the pastry on a lightly floured work surface to a large rectangle, a little bigger than the surface of the dish. Slice 4 × 1cm (½in) strips from the pastry. Wet the edges of the dish with water and stick the four strips of pastry to the edges. Wet the top of the strips, then carefully lay the large sheet of pastry over the top. Press around the edges so it sticks to the strips. Trim then crimp the edges. Use a small sharp knife to make two holes in the pastry, one either side of the inverted cup or pie funnel, to allow the steam to escape and prevent the pastry from becoming soggy.

8. Roll out the trimmings of pastry into a long rectangle. Chill in the freezer until very firm, then carefully cut out the letters PIE. Brush the pie pastry with the beaten egg, then stick the letters to the top and brush again. Bake in the centre of the preheated oven for about 45 minutes until golden.

Horseradish Beef and
Red Pepper Stir-fry

**A quick and special meal using sirloin steak. If you prefer fillet steak,
that would also be perfect for this recipe, as it is quick cooking.
This sauce is quite fiery – add less horseradish, if liked.**

Serves 4

3 tbsp sunflower oil

400g (14oz) sirloin
beef, sliced into
thin strips

2 large banana shallots,
thinly sliced

2 red peppers,
deseeded and sliced

250g (9oz) chestnut
mushrooms,
thickly sliced

1 large garlic clove,
finely grated

150g (5oz) baby
spinach

3 tbsp hot horseradish
from a jar

Mary's Tips

Best made and served.

Not suitable for freezing.

1. Heat 2 tablespoons of the sunflower oil in a large frying pan
   over a high heat. Season the beef with salt and freshly ground
   black pepper and brown for a minute on each side until
   sealed, but still pink in the centre. You will need to do this
   in batches. Remove from the pan and set aside.

2. Add the remaining oil and shallots to the pan and fry over
   a medium heat for 5 minutes, until nearly soft. Increase the
   heat, add the peppers and mushrooms and fry over a high
   heat for 2–3 minutes. Add the garlic and fry for about 30
   seconds. Add the spinach and fry for a minute until wilted.

3. Return the beef to the pan, including the juices, and stir in
   the horseradish. Heat through, check the seasoning and serve
   at once.

Rack of Lamb with Roasted Vegetables and Mint Dressing

This is a smart dish for when you are hosting but is so easy to make. The vibrant colour of the squash and spinach make this look so fresh. The layer of fat on top of the lamb should be removed using a sharp knife, so you are left with only a very thin layer. This is to prevent there being too much fat when browning.

Serves 4

1 × 7-bone rack of lamb, French-trimmed
2 garlic cloves, quartered

For the roasted vegetables
1 small butternut squash, peeled and cubed (650g/ 1lb 7oz prepared weight)
1 red pepper, cut into 2cm/¾in cubes
1 onion, thickly sliced
3 tbsp olive oil
115g (4oz) baby spinach, roughly chopped

For the mint dressing
Bunch of mint, leaves chopped
2 tbsp white wine vinegar
1 tbsp caster sugar
6 tbsp olive oil
2 tsp Dijon mustard

Mary's Tips

The dressing can be made up to 4 hours ahead. The first roasting of vegetables and browning the lamb can be done up to 3 hours ahead.

Not suitable for freezing.

1. Preheat the oven to 220°C/200°C Fan/Gas 7.

2. Arrange the squash, pepper and onion in a large roasting tin. Add the oil and season with salt and freshly ground black pepper. Stir to coat the vegetables in the oil, then roast in the preheated oven for about 15 minutes.

3. Remove any excess fat from the top of the lamb. Score the thin layer of fat in a crisscross pattern and season well. Make 8 holes in the fat and push the garlic pieces into the holes. Heat a frying pan until hot over a high heat. Add the lamb, fat-side down, and fry until brown. Brown the meat on all sides, then set aside.

4. Remove the tin from the oven and push the vegetables to one side. Place the browned rack of lamb, fat-side up, on the cleared side of the tin and roast in the oven for about 15 minutes (the lamb will be pink). Transfer the lamb to a carving board, cover with foil and set aside to rest for 5 minutes.

5. Mix the ingredients for the mint dressing together in a small saucepan with 2 tablespoons water. Warm over a low heat.

6. Place the roasting tin of vegetables over a low heat. Remove any excess fat from the tin, then add the spinach. Gently fold the spinach into the hot vegetables to wilt (it should still be bright green), then pour over half the warm dressing.

7. Carve the lamb and arrange on a plate with the vegetables. Drizzle the remaining dressing over the lamb to serve.

Slow-cooked Spiced Lamb

Cooked for a few hours, this tender lamb dish has Lebanese-style spices and chickpeas. It is very aromatic rather than hot and spicy.

Serves 6

2 tbsp sunflower oil

1kg (2lb 4oz) lamb neck fillet, cut into 5cm (2in) cubes

3 large onions, sliced

3 large garlic cloves, finely grated

2 tbsp ground coriander

2 tsp allspice

1 tbsp ground cinnamon

3 tbsp tomato purée

200ml (⅓ pint) white wine

300ml (½ pint) beef or chicken stock

150g (5oz) ready-to-eat dried apricots, halved

1 tbsp honey

1 × 400g tin chickpeas, drained and rinsed

Juice of ½ lemon

Small bunch of coriander, leaves roughly chopped

Mary's Tips

Can be made up to a day ahead.

Freezes well without the chickpeas.

1. Preheat the oven to 160°C/140°C Fan/Gas 3.

2. Heat the oil in a deep frying pan with a lid over a high heat. Add the lamb and fry in batches until browned. Remove the lamb from the pan and set aside.

3. Add the onions and garlic to the same unwashed pan and fry for about 5 minutes. Sprinkle in all the spices and the tomato purée and stir for a few seconds. Pour in the wine and stock and bring up to the boil.

4. Return the lamb to the pan and add the apricots, honey and chickpeas. Season well with salt and freshly ground black pepper. Cover the pan with a lid, transfer to the preheated oven and cook for about 2 hours until tender.

5. Add the lemon juice and fresh coriander and check the seasoning before serving with couscous or Bay and Lemon Brown Rice (see page 204).

Rugby Lamb

Heart-warming lamb stew, serve it with rice or mashed potato or celeriac. You can use neck fillet or leg or shoulder for this recipe. Luce made this for a gang of friends when the rugby world cup match was on, hence the title!

Serves 4–6

2 tbsp sunflower oil

750g (1lb 10oz) lamb shoulder, trimmed and diced into 5cm (2in) cubes (prepared weight)

3 thin leeks, thickly sliced

1 red pepper, deseeded and sliced into large chunks

3 garlic cloves, finely grated

¼ tsp cayenne pepper

2 tsp ground cumin

500g (1lb 2oz) passata

100ml (3½fl oz) water or stock

2 tsp balsamic glaze

150g (5oz) baby spinach leaves

Mary's Tips

Can be made up to a day ahead without the spinach. Reheat to serve and add the spinach before serving.

Freezes well without the spinach.

1. Preheat the oven to 160°C/140°C Fan/Gas 3.

2. Heat a large ovenproof frying pan or flameproof casserole over a high heat until hot. Add the oil and fry the lamb in batches until golden and sealed. Set aside.

3. Add the leeks and pepper to the pan and fry for 3–4 minutes, until starting to soften a little. Add the garlic, sprinkle over the spices and fry for 10 seconds.

4. Stir in the passata and water or stock, and return the lamb to the pan. Season with salt and freshly ground black pepper and bring up to the boil. Cover with a lid and transfer to the oven for 2 hours until tender.

5. Remove from the oven and add the balsamic glaze and spinach. Cover with a lid for 30 seconds, then stir until the spinach has just wilted.

6. Check the seasoning and serve piping hot with rice or mash.

Duck Breast with Brandy and Watercress Sauce

A real winner for a special occasion. The sauce can be made ahead and the watercress added just before serving. Duck breasts can be browned ahead, then oven roasted for 10–12 minutes, according to size, just before serving. The duck breast skin can be rendered down and used for roast potatoes.

Serves 4

4 duck breasts, skin removed
2 tbsp runny honey
1 tbsp sunflower oil
Knob of butter

For the brandy and watercress sauce
75g (3oz) watercress
Knob of butter
2 large banana shallots, finely chopped
4 tbsp brandy
300ml (½ pint) pouring double cream
Good dash of Worcestershire sauce
1 tbsp Dijon mustard
Juice of ½ lemon

Mary's Tips

To prepare ahead, brown the duck breasts for 2 minutes on each side, then place in the fridge until needed. Bring the duck up to room temperature, then roast at 200°C/180°C Fan/Gas 6 for 12 minutes. Make the sauce up to a day ahead, but add the chopped watercress after reheating.

Not suitable for freezing.

1. Preheat the oven to 200°C/180°C Fan/Gas 6. Line a baking sheet with non-stick baking paper.

2. Season the duck breasts with salt and freshly ground black pepper, then drizzle with the runny honey.

3. Place a frying pan over a high heat until hot. Add the oil and butter. When the butter is foaming, add the duck and fry for about 2 minutes on each side. Transfer to the prepared baking sheet and roast in the oven for about 8–10 minutes, depending on the size of the breasts. Remove from the oven, set aside on a hot plate, cover with foil and leave to rest for 10 minutes.

4. Meanwhile, make the sauce. Set a few pieces of watercress aside for garnish, then chop the remainder. Melt the butter in a frying pan over a medium heat. Add the shallots and fry for 3–4 minutes. Add the brandy and reduce over a high heat. Add the cream, Worcestershire sauce, Dijon mustard and seasoning. Boil for 1 minute, then add the lemon juice, chopped watercress and any duck juices. Reduce the heat and simmer for 1 minute.

5. Carve the duck into slices and serve with the sauce and some fresh watercress on the side.

Venison and Bacon Burgers

Minced venison is becoming less exclusive and more readily available in butchers and supermarkets. These burgers are full of flavour. Redcurrant jelly is traditional to serve with venison, but you can choose other condiments, if you prefer, and you could serve them without the bun.

Makes 6 small burgers

6 cream crackers

2 rashers smoked bacon, roughly chopped

1 small onion, roughly chopped

300g (10½oz) minced venison

1 tbsp tomato purée

A few drops of Worcestershire sauce

4 tbsp freshly chopped parsley

Sunflower oil, for frying

To serve

6 small brioche buns

6 tsp redcurrant jelly

6 tsp mayonnaise

6 lettuce leaves

A few pickled gherkins, sliced

Mary's Tips

Burgers can be made and kept raw in the fridge up to 2 days ahead.

Burgers freeze well raw.

1. Place the crackers in a bag and finely crush them using a rolling pin.

2. Place the bacon and onion in a food processor and whiz for a few seconds. Add the venison, tomato purée, Worcestershire sauce and parsley, and season with salt and freshly ground black pepper. Whiz until finely chopped.

3. Add the crushed crackers to the mixture and process to combine. Shape into 6 small burgers.

4. Heat a little oil in a frying pan over a high heat until hot. Add the burgers and fry for about 3 minutes on each side until golden and cooked through (they should be a little pink inside).

5. Meanwhile, toast the brioche buns and spread with redcurrant jelly and mayonnaise. Place a lettuce leaf on top, then the burgers and sliced gherkins, and sandwich together to serve.

Venison Steaks with Glazed Beets and Little Gem Salad

Venison is a lean and healthy red meat, which is getting more and more popular. I love it. Venison is traditionally served with redcurrant jelly and we've used it here to glaze the beetroot.

Serves 4

2–3 tbsp olive oil

450g (1lb) cooked beetroot, chopped into 1cm (½in) cubes

1 tbsp redcurrant jelly

2 Little Gem lettuces, torn into bite-sized pieces

4 × 115g (4oz) venison steaks (loin fillet)

Knob of butter

For the salad dressing

3 tbsp full-fat mayonnaise

2 tbsp hot horseradish sauce

Juice of ½ lemon

Mary's Tips

Beets can be cooked up to 6 hours ahead and reheated and glazed to serve. Little Gem salad dressing can be made up to 2 days ahead.

Not suitable for freezing.

1. Heat 2 tablespoons of the olive oil in a large non-stick frying pan over a medium heat. Add the beetroot cubes and season with salt and freshly ground black pepper. Fry for about 15–20 minutes, stirring occasionally, until the beetroot is cooked, but still with a little bite. Remove from the heat and add the redcurrant jelly. Stir to coat and set aside.

2. To make the salad dressing, measure the mayonnaise, horseradish and lemon juice into a large bowl. Mix well and season. Add the torn lettuce and toss to coat in the dressing.

3. Place the venison steaks on a board. Brush with the remaining oil and season.

4. Place a frying pan over a high heat until hot. Add the steaks and fry for about 2–3 minutes on each side, depending on the thickness of the steaks. Add the butter at the end of the cooking time and spoon over the meat. Transfer the steaks to a plate, cover with foil and leave to rest for a few minutes.

5. Carve the steaks into slices, place on warm plates and serve with the beetroot and salad.

Veggie

Crumble-topped Veggie Pie

Hearty and warming roasted veg with a little blue cheese for added flavour. If Dolcelatte cheese isn't available, use any other blue cheese, such as Stilton or gorgonzola.

Serves 6

1 small butternut
squash, peeled,
deseeded and cut
into large cubes
(600g/1lb 5oz
prepared weight)

2 large sweet potatoes,
peeled and cut into
3cm (1¼in) cubes
(300g/10½oz)
prepared weight)

1 large red pepper,
deseeded and
cut into 3cm
(1¼in) cubes

1 small onion, cut
into wedges

2 tbsp olive oil

2 tbsp sun-dried
tomato paste

1 garlic clove,
finely grated

150g (5oz) Dolcelatte
cheese, cut
into pieces

For the crumble

175g (6oz) plain flour

115g (4oz) butter,
cubed

75g (3oz) Parmesan,
grated

2 tbsp freshly
chopped parsley

1. Preheat the oven to 220°C/200°C Fan/Gas 7.

2. Arrange all the vegetables in a large roasting tin. Add the olive oil and season with salt and freshly ground black pepper. Toss together to coat the vegetables in the oil. Roast in the preheated oven for about 30–35 minutes, until lightly golden, turning halfway through. Set aside.

3. Mix the sun-dried tomato paste and garlic together in a small bowl. Spoon the vegetables into an ovenproof dish and blob the cheese and the tomato paste mixture over the top.

4. To make the crumble, measure the flour and butter into a mixing bowl. Rub in the butter using your fingertips until the mixture resembles breadcrumbs. Add the Parmesan, parsley and season.

5. Scatter the crumble over the top of the vegetables and bake in the preheated oven for about 30–35 minutes, until golden and crispy on top.

Mary's Tips

Can be made and assembled up to 8 hours ahead.

Freezes well.

Cheese Fondue

There's nothing more indulgent than cheese fondue on a cold winter's day. Perfect for the young or for sitting round a fire.

Serves 6

200ml (⅓ pint) dry
  white wine
1 tbsp lemon juice
200g (7oz) Gruyère,
  grated
200g (7oz) Emmental,
  grated
1 tbsp cornflour
1 tbsp kirsch

To serve
Crusty bread
Small boiled new
  potatoes
Vegetable crudités
Gherkins

Mary's Tips

*Fondue can be made
up to 2 hours ahead.
Add a touch of
milk to loosen when
reheating, if too thick.*

Not suitable for freezing.

1. Pour the wine and lemon juice into a heavy-based saucepan over a medium–low heat and warm until steaming. Add the cheeses, a handful at a time, whisking between each addition, until all the cheese has been incorporated. Continue to stir for 4–5 minutes until everything is fully melted, smooth and creamy.

2. Mix the cornflour with the kirsch in a small bowl. Stir this into the cheese mixture and continue to cook over a low heat for 1 minute, until thickened and smooth.

3. Serve immediately with crusty bread, boiled new potatoes, vegetable crudités and cornichons. You can place the fondue back over a low heat, if you need to reheat it after serving.

Fennel and Onion Tart Tatin

A delicious tart with a caramelised top and a puff pastry base. Be careful to keep the whole round rings of onion flat, so they maintain their shape. This also works well in a 23cm (9in) springform cake tin. After adding the onion to the garlic and glaze, carefully spoon into the base of the cake tin and continue to assemble.

Serves 6

2 large bulbs fennel, halved and thickly sliced

2 large onions, sliced into thick rings, keeping them whole

55g (2oz) butter

3 garlic cloves, finely grated

25g (1oz) light muscovado sugar

1 tbsp freshly chopped sage, plus 8 whole leaves

2 tbsp balsamic glaze, plus 1 tsp to drizzle

1 × 320g packet ready-rolled puff pastry

55g (2oz) Parmesan, finely grated

2–3 tbsp olive oil

Mary's Tips

Can be made up to 4 hours ahead.

Not suitable for freezing.

1. Preheat the oven to 220°C/200°C Fan/Gas 7. You will need a shallow 23cm (9in) ovenproof frying pan.

2. Bring a saucepan of water to the boil. Add the fennel and boil for 2 minutes. Add the onions and boil for 3–4 minutes, until nearly soft. Drain well, keeping the onion rings whole, if possible.

3. Melt the butter in the ovenproof frying pan over a medium heat. Add the garlic and sugar and fry for 30 seconds, then stir in the chopped sage. Arrange the onions in a single layer, then place the fennel on top and season with salt and freshly ground black pepper. Drizzle with 2 tablespoons balsamic glaze and fry for about 5 minutes, until the sugar starts to turn the onions golden brown. Turn off the heat and leave to cool in the pan.

4. Roll out the pastry on a lightly floured work surface to a slightly larger rectangle. Cut a round of pastry the size of the pan.

5. Sprinkle on the Parmesan and place the pastry on top. Bake in the preheated oven for about 20–25 minutes, until golden brown. Remove from the oven and set aside for 10 minutes.

6. Meanwhile, fry the whole sage leaves in a small frying pan over a high heat with 1–2 tablespoons olive oil for about 30 seconds until crisp. Remove from the pan and place on kitchen paper to drain the excess oil. Sprinkle with sea salt.

7. Carefully turn the tart upside down onto a plate. Mix 1 tablespoon of olive oil with 1 teaspoon balsamic glaze and use to brush the top of the tart.

8. Scatter over the sage leaves and cut into wedges to serve hot.

Spiced Aubergine and Fresh Tomato Spaghetti

A healthy and delicious midweek supper – full of flavour and a little spice.

Serves 6

6 large ripe tomatoes

2 aubergines, diced into
  2cm (¾in) cubes

6 tbsp olive oil

2 tsp ground coriander

1 large banana shallot,
  finely chopped

2 large garlic cloves,
  finely grated

1 red chilli, deseeded
  and finely diced

2 heaped tbsp
  tomato purée

1 tsp caster sugar

250g (9oz) spaghetti

Knob of butter

Small bunch of parsley,
  leaves chopped

Mary's Tips

Best made and served.

Not for freezing.

1. Preheat the oven to 200°C/180°C Fan/Gas 6.

2. Skin the tomatoes by scoring the bases with a cross and placing them in boiling water. Leave for 30 seconds, then drain and refresh under cold water. Starting from the cross on the base, peel the skin away then roughly chop the tomatoes.

3. Arrange the aubergine cubes in a large roasting tin and brush with 2 tablespoons of the olive oil. Season with salt and freshly ground black pepper and sprinkle over the ground coriander. Toss the aubergine to coat in the oil and spice, then place in the preheated oven to roast for about 20–25 minutes, until golden. Set aside.

4. Meanwhile, heat the remaining oil in a large frying pan over a medium heat. Add the shallot and fry for 2 minutes. Add the garlic and chilli and fry for 30 seconds. Add the skinned tomatoes and fry for a few minutes. Stir in the tomato purée and sugar. Reduce the heat and cook the sauce gently for a few minutes.

5. Cook the spaghetti in boiling salted water according to the packet instructions. Drain, reserving 4 tablespoons of the cooking water, and add the spaghetti to the pan with the tomatoes. Stir in the reserved pasta water, aubergines, butter and parsley. Toss everything together.

6. Check the seasoning and serve at once.

Veggie Penne Bake

This is very much like the Penne Bolognaise Bake on page 114 but it is a vegetable version. You could make one of each for a large dinner party.

page 114

Serves 6

175g (6oz) penne pasta

For the vegetables
2 tbsp olive oil
1 large onion,
  roughly chopped
2 red peppers,
  deseeded and diced
500g (1lb 2oz) chestnut
  mushrooms, sliced
2 garlic cloves,
  finely grated
2 × 400g tins chopped
  tomatoes
2 tbsp tomato purée
Small bunch of basil,
  leaves chopped

For the cheese sauce
25g (1oz) butter
25g (1oz) plain flour
450ml (¾ pint)
  hot milk
2 tsp Dijon mustard
55g (2oz) Parmesan,
  coarsely grated
115g (4oz) Cheddar,
  coarsely grated

Mary's Tips

*Can be assembled up
to 12 hours ahead.*

Freezes well.

1. Preheat the oven to 200°C/180°C Fan/Gas 6. You will need a large 23 × 28cm (9 × 11in) ovenproof dish.

2. To make the vegetable layer, heat the oil in a deep frying pan over a high heat. Add the onion and peppers and fry for 5–8 minutes. Add the mushrooms and garlic and fry until the liquid has evaporated from the mushrooms. Stir in the chopped tomatoes, tomato purée and basil. Cover with a lid, bring up to the boil, then reduce the heat and simmer for about 12–15 minutes, until slightly reduced. Season well with salt and freshly ground black pepper.

3. Meanwhile, cook the pasta in boiling salted water according to the packet instructions. Drain and refresh under cold water. Drain again.

4. To make the cheese sauce, melt the butter in a saucepan over a high heat. Add the flour and stir for a few seconds. Whisk in the hot milk, whisking until smooth and thickened. Add the mustard and Parmesan and season well.

5. Spoon the vegetables into the base of the ovenproof dish. Top with the pasta and spread out to an even layer. Spoon the cheese sauce over the pasta and sprinkle with the Cheddar. Bake in the preheated oven for about 25–30 minutes until bubbling.

6. Serve piping hot with a green leaf salad.

Mushroom, Basil
and Broccoli Pappardelle

**The perfect midweek supper dish. It is important to keep the slices of
mushroom large; if they are too small, they will get lost among the pasta.**

Serves 6

Knob of butter

2 tbsp olive oil

3 garlic cloves,
  finely grated

250g (9oz) chestnut
  mushrooms,
  thickly sliced

250g (9oz) Portobello
  mushrooms,
  thickly sliced

250g (9oz) shitake
  mushrooms,
  thickly sliced

350g (12oz)
  pappardelle pasta

200g (7oz) tenderstem
  broccoli

200ml (⅓ pint) pouring
  double cream

3 egg yolks

125g (4½oz) Parmesan,
  coarsely grated

1 large bunch of basil,
  leaves chopped

Mary's Tips

Best made and served.

Not suitable for freezing

1. Melt the butter and oil in a large frying pan over a medium heat. Add the garlic and fry for a few seconds. Add all the mushrooms and toss over the heat until just starting to brown. Season well with salt and freshly ground black pepper and set the pan aside.

2. Cook the pasta in salted boiling water according to the packet instructions. Three minutes before the end of the cooking time, add the broccoli. Drain the pasta and broccoli, reserving 6 tablespoons of the pasta water.

3. Meanwhile, place the cream, egg yolks and Parmesan in a small bowl and beat together with a fork.

4. Add the pasta, broccoli and pasta water to the pan with the mushrooms and stir over a gentle heat. Pour in the cream and egg mixture, season well and stir to coat.

5. Toss in the basil and serve piping hot in a wide-rimmed bowl with green salad leaves on the side.

Lentil and Artichoke Romano Peppers

A lovely vegetarian dish that would make a great starter, light lunch or supper. This is an interesting way to cook halloumi and we find it works really well with the soft artichokes and lentils.

Makes 6 halves

Sunflower oil,
  for greasing
250g (9oz) cooked puy
  lentils from a packet
¼–½ red chilli,
  finely diced
1 bunch of spring
  onions, trimmed
  and finely chopped
3 tbsp sun-dried
  tomato paste
115g (4oz) artichokes
  in oil, drained
  and chopped
150g (5oz) halloumi,
  grated
3 large Romano
  peppers, halved,
  keeping the
  stalk attached,
  and deseeded

Mary's Tips

*Can be assembled up
to 4 hours ahead.*

Not suitable for freezing.

1. Preheat the oven to 200°C/180°C Fan/Gas 6. Grease a roasting tin with oil.

2. Heat the lentils according to the packet instructions, then tip into a large bowl. Add the chilli, spring onions, sun-dried tomato paste, artichokes and three-quarters of the halloumi. Mix well and season with salt and freshly ground black pepper.

3. Divide the filling between the pepper halves and arrange them in the prepared roasting tin. Sprinkle over the remaining cheese and bake in the oven for about 20–25 minutes, until the peppers have softened and the cheese is golden on top.

Falafel with Pickled Red Cabbage and Whipped Feta

These are a coarse falafel with a little spice and lots of herbs. The pickled cabbage is so healthy and improves with age. Whipping the feta gives a lovely light spread to go with the patties.

Serves 6

2–3 tbsp olive oil

2 large banana shallots, finely chopped

2 garlic cloves, finely grated

1 tbsp ground coriander

2 tsp ground cumin

Finely grated zest and juice of 1 lemon

Small bunch of parsley, leaves roughly chopped

Small bunch of coriander, leaves roughly chopped

4 tbsp plain flour

1 egg, beaten

2 × 400g tins chickpeas, drained and rinsed

2 Little Gem lettuces, shredded

For the pickled cabbage

4 tbsp white wine vinegar

25g (1oz) caster sugar

225g (8oz) red cabbage, finely shredded

½ red onion, finely sliced

1. First make the pickled cabbage. Add the vinegar and sugar to a small saucepan and place over a medium heat. Stir until the sugar has dissolved. Pour the syrup into a bowl and add the cabbage and sliced onion. Toss to coat in the syrup and season to taste with salt. Cover and leave for 1 hour.

2. Meanwhile, place 2 tablespoons of the oil in a frying pan over a high heat. Add the shallots and fry for a few minutes, until soft and tinged brown. Add the garlic and spices and fry for 10 seconds. Leave to cool.

3. Tip the cooled onion mixture into a large bowl and stir in the lemon zest and juice, the fresh herbs, flour and beaten egg.

4. Meanwhile, tip the drained chickpeas into a food processor and whiz until finely chopped (but still with texture). Add the chickpeas to the bowl with the herb mixture and season well with salt and freshly ground black pepper. Mix everything together, using your hands, and squeeze the mixture to come together. Shape into 12 oval or round patties. Leave to chill in the fridge for 30 minutes.

5. To make the whipped feta, add the ingredients to a food processor and blend for 30 seconds.

6. Heat the remaining oil in a large frying pan over a high heat. Fry the falafels for 3 minutes on each side until lightly browned. You may need to do this in batches.

For the whipped feta
200g (7oz) feta cheese
6 tbsp Greek yoghurt

7. Divide the lettuce between six plates and top with 2 falafels, a pile of cabbage and a spoonful of whipped feta cheese. Otherwise, place everything on a sharing platter.

Mary's Tips

Falafels can be made up to a day ahead. Pickle can be made up to 2 days ahead.

Freeze well uncooked.

Fast Quiche

**What a cheat this is! Supper in the evening, kids popping in, don't know what
to make . . . here we go! The word tortilla is Spanish and fajita is Mexican, but
to me it's called a wrap! Buy large ones so they fit up the sides of the tin.**

Serves 4

1 tbsp sunflower
    oil, plus extra
    for greasing
1 large tortilla wrap
1 large onion,
    finely chopped
150g (5oz) chestnut
    mushrooms, sliced
75g (3oz) mature
    Cheddar, grated
2 eggs, beaten
200ml (⅓ pint) pouring
    double cream
2 tbsp freshly
    chopped parsley

Mary's Tips

Best made and served.

Not suitable for freezing.

1. Preheat the oven to 200°C/180°C Fan/Gas 6. You will need
   a 20cm (8in) loose-bottomed sandwich tin, brushed with oil.
   Place a heavy baking sheet in the oven to get hot.

2. Lay the wrap inside the sandwich tin to cover the base and
   to go halfway up the sides. Press firmly to the sides of the tin.

3. To make the filling, place the oil in a large frying pan over a
   medium heat. Add the onion and fry for a few minutes, then
   cover with a lid and cook for 10 minutes until soft. Add the
   mushrooms and fry for a few minutes. Drain off any liquid.

4. Spoon the onion and mushrooms into the wrap-lined tin
   and spread evenly. Sprinkle half the cheese over the top.

5. Beat the eggs and cream together in a small bowl. Season
   with salt and freshly ground black pepper and add the
   remaining cheese and the parsley to the egg mixture. Pour
   over the mushroom filling. Place the tin on the hot baking
   sheet in the preheated oven and cook for about 25 minutes,
   until set and lightly golden.

6. Leave for stand for 5 minutes, then serve hot in wedges with
   a dressed tomato salad.

Cauliflower and Sweet Potato Curry

A great veggie curry. Serve it on its own with basmati rice or as part of a curry party with Super Easy Mango Chicken on page 84.

Serves 6

2 tbsp sunflower oil

2 large onions, finely sliced

Large piece of fresh root ginger, finely grated

2 garlic cloves, finely grated

½ red chilli, deseeded and finely diced

150g (5oz) carrots, cut into 2cm (¾in) cubes

300g (10½oz) sweet potatoes, peeled and cut into 2cm (¾in) cubes

2 tbsp medium curry powder

1 tsp ground turmeric

2 tsp ground cumin

2 tbsp tomato purée

4 large tomatoes, each cut into 6

1 × 400g tin chopped tomatoes

600ml (1 pint) vegetable stock

350g (12oz) cauliflower, broken into florets

150g (5oz) green beans, each sliced into 3

1. Heat the oil in a large frying pan over a high heat. Add the onions and fry for 3–4 minutes. Add the ginger, garlic and chilli and fry for a few seconds. Add the carrots, sweet potatoes and spices and fry for 30 seconds. Stir in the tomato purée, fresh and chopped tomatoes, and the stock. Season with salt and freshly ground black pepper, cover with a lid and bring up to the boil. Reduce the heat and simmer for about 10 minutes, until the sweet potatoes are nearly cooked.

2. Add the cauliflower, cover with a lid and cook for about 8 minutes, until the vegetables are tender but still with a little bite.

3. Meanwhile, cook the green beans in boiling water for 3 minutes. Drain and stir into the curry.

4. Serve with rice and mango chutney on the side.

Mary's Tips

Can be made up to a day ahead. Add the green beans just before serving.

Freezes well without the beans.

Lasagne Aubergine Melanzane

A simple and delicious vegetarian lasagne using the classic flavours of *Melanzane Parmigiana*. It's more healthy, too, as there is no white sauce and only one layer of pasta. All in one dish.

Serves 6–8

3 aubergines, sliced lengthways into 1cm (½in) slices

3–4 tbsp olive oil

2 large onions, finely chopped

4 garlic cloves, finely grated

1× 400g tin chopped tomatoes

1 × 500g carton passata

2 tbsp sun-dried tomato paste

1 tbsp freshly chopped oregano

1 small bunch of basil, leaves roughly chopped

3 fresh or dried lasagne sheets

250g (9oz) mozzarella, broken into pieces

115g (4oz) Parmesan, coarsely grated

Mary's Tips

Can be assembled up to 8 hours ahead.

Freezes well.

1. Preheat the oven to 220°C/200°C Fan/Gas 7. Line two large baking sheets with non-stick baking paper. You will need a 1.75-litre (3-pint) wide-based, shallow ovenproof dish.

2. Arrange the aubergines on the prepared baking sheets, brush with oil and season well with salt and freshly ground black pepper. Roast in the preheated oven for about 20–25 minutes until golden and soft. Remove from the oven and set aside.

3. Reduce the oven temperature to 200°C/180°C Fan/Gas 6.

4. Heat 2 tablespoons of oil in a deep frying pan over a high heat. Add the onions and fry for 5 minutes, stirring. Add the garlic and fry for 1 minute. Pour in the tomatoes, passata and sun-dried tomato paste, lower the heat and simmer for 5 minutes. Add the fresh herbs and season well.

5. Soak the lasagne sheets in a shallow dish of boiling water for 5 minutes, then drain.

6. Divide the tomato sauce into four and divide each pile of cheese into four. Spoon one portion of sauce into the base of the ovenproof dish and spread to the corners. Scatter one portion each of the mozzarella and Parmesan on top, then lay half the aubergine slices on the cheeses. Spoon a portion of the sauce on top, then add the sheets of lasagne, followed by another portion of the cheeses. Top with another portion of sauce, then the remaining aubergine slices and another portion of the cheeses. Finally, spoon on the remaining sauce and arrange the remaining cheeses in piles on top. Bake in the preheated oven for about 30 minutes, until bubbling and golden.

7. Serve hot with dressed salad leaves.

Miso Aubergine
with Lentil and Veggie Stir-fry

This is a triumph! Not only does it look amazing, it tastes twice as good. The miso paste not only gives flavour but adds a golden glaze to the aubergine, too.

Serves 4

2 heaped tbsp white miso paste

3 tbsp sweet chilli sauce

1 tsp grated fresh root ginger

2 aubergines

2 tbsp sunflower oil

1 bunch of spring onions, trimmed and sliced

1 red pepper, deseeded and sliced into julienne strips

2 carrots, sliced into julienne strips

1 garlic clove, finely grated

250g (9oz) cooked Puy lentils from a packet

2 tbsp soy sauce

Small bunch of coriander, leaves roughly chopped

Mary's Tips

Vegetables can all be prepared ahead and ready to go but best made and served.

Not suitable for freezing.

1. Preheat the oven to 200°C/180°C Fan/Gas 6.

2. Mix the miso paste, 2 tablespoons of the sweet chilli sauce, 2 tablespoons of water and the fresh root ginger together in a small bowl.

3. Slice the aubergines in half lengthways and score the flesh into diagonal cubes, cutting down to the skin but not through it. Brush the miso mixture over the surface of the aubergines and season with salt and freshly ground black pepper. Place the aubergines in a roasting tin so they fit snugly and add 3 tablespoons of water to the tin. Cover the tin with foil and bake in the preheated oven for 30 minutes. Remove the foil and bake for a further 10–15 minutes, until the aubergines are soft and golden brown.

4. Heat the oil in a large frying pan over a high heat. Add the spring onions, pepper and carrots and fry for 4–5 minutes. Add the garlic and fry for 30 seconds. Add the Puy lentils, soy sauce, coriander and the remaining sweet chilli sauce. Season well.

5. Spoon the lentils and vegetables onto a platter and arrange the aubergines on top. Serve half an aubergine per person.

Brown Rice and Squash Stir-fry

Delicious as a meal in itself or with the Sticky Chicken Bites on page 32.

Delicious as a meal in itself or with the Sticky Chicken Bites on page 32.

Serves 4

2 tbsp olive oil

1 large onion, finely chopped

1 red pepper, deseeded and finely diced

350g (12oz) butternut squash, peeled and diced into 1cm (½in) cubes (prepared weight)

2 tsp finely grated fresh root ginger

55g (2oz) petits pois

1 × 250g packet cooked brown basmati rice

2 tbsp soy sauce

Mary's Tips

Best made and served.

Not suitable for freezing.

1. Heat the oil in a large frying pan over a medium heat. Add the onion, pepper and squash and fry for about 8–10 minutes, stirring, until the vegetables are cooked. Add the ginger and peas and fry for 1 minute.

2. Heat the rice according to the packet instructions, then add to the pan with the vegetables. Toss over the heat. Add the soy and some freshly ground black pepper and mix well.

3. Serve piping hot in bowls.

Leek and Gruyère Tart with Parmesan and Chive Pastry

A simple and classic tart. The ideal midweek supper for a special occasion.

Serves 6–8

For the Parmesan and chive pastry
225g (8oz) plain flour
115g (4oz) butter
25g (1oz) Parmesan, grated
1 tbsp freshly snipped chives
1 egg, beaten

For the filling
Knob of butter
2 tbsp olive oil
3 leeks, thinly sliced
5 eggs
450ml (¾ pint) pouring double cream
200g (7oz) Gruyère cheese, coarsely grated

You will need a 28cm (11in) deep fluted loose-bottomed tart tin.

Mary's Tips

Can be made up to a day ahead.

Freezes well.

1. To make the pastry, measure the flour, butter and Parmesan into a food processor. Whiz until breadcrumb stage. Add the chives and a little salt and freshly ground black pepper. Beat the egg with 1 tablespoon of water, then pour into the processor and whiz until the pastry comes together. Gently knead into a ball.

2. Roll the pastry out on a lightly floured work surface until thin. Use to line the tart tin, then prick the base with a fork. Chill in the fridge for 30 minutes.

3. Meanwhile, preheat the oven to 200°C/180°C Fan/Gas 6.

4. Line the pastry with non-stick baking paper and fill with baking beans. Blind bake the pastry in the preheated oven for about 15 minutes, then remove the paper and beans and cook for another 5–10 minutes, until lightly golden. Trim the edges of the pastry case to neaten.

5. To make the filling, melt the butter and oil in a frying pan over a low heat. Add the leeks and fry gently until soft. Set aside to cool. Beat the eggs and cream together in a bowl or jug, stir in three-quarters of the cheese and season well.

6. Spoon the cooked leeks into the base of the tart. Carefully pour in the egg and cream mixture. Sprinkle the remaining cheese on top and cook in the preheated oven for about 25–30 minutes, until the top is lightly golden and the mixture is just set in the middle.

7. Stand for 10 minutes, then cut into slices and serve warm.

Salads and Sides

Kitchen Garden Grain Salad

A great go-to salad, with a delicious garlic and lemon dressing. For ease, you can now buy precooked lentils, rice and quinoa – they make for a quick and easy salad.

Serves 4–6

1 × 250g packet cooked puy lentils

1 × 250g packet cooked mixed red and white quinoa

2 medium carrots, peeled and coarsely grated

5 spring onions, sliced

2 large tomatoes, deseeded and cut into 2cm (¾in) cubes

½ cucumber, deseeded and finely diced

½ bunch of parsley, leaves roughly chopped

55g (2oz) pumpkin seeds

For the dressing

Zest and juice of 2 large lemons

2 tbsp white wine vinegar

6 tbsp olive oil

1 garlic clove, finely grated

2–3 tbsp sweet chilli sauce

1. Heat the lentils and quinoa according to the packet instructions. Tip into a large bowl and leave to cool.

2. Mix all the dressing ingredients together in a jug.

3. Add the carrots, spring onions, tomatoes, cucumber, parsley and seeds to the bowl with the lentils and quinoa.

4. Pour the dressing over the salad and season well with salt and freshly ground black pepper. Toss everything together and serve.

Mary's Tips

Can be assembled up to 6 hours ahead. Dress to serve.

Not suitable for freezing.

Pan-fried Halloumi and Vegetable Salad with Herb Dressing

A feast of a salad with pan-fried halloumi and a mustard herb dressing. Be careful not to overcook the halloumi, as it becomes tough and squeaky!

Serves 6

2 tbsp olive oil

2 courgettes, sliced in long thin strips, skin on

2 red peppers, deseeded and sliced into thick slices

4 large tomatoes

1 large cos lettuce, sliced widthways

115g (4oz) pitted soft black olives

2 tbsp each freshly chopped mint, dill, chives and parsley

250g (9oz) halloumi cheese, sliced horizontally into 3 pieces

For the herb dressing

2 tsp Dijon mustard

2 tbsp white wine vinegar

8 tbsp sunflower oil

2 tbsp runny honey

Squeeze of lemon

Mary's Tips

Can be assembled up to 2 hours ahead. Dress just before serving. Halloumi is best pan-fried to serve.

Not suitable for freezing.

1. Measure a tablespoon of the olive oil into a large bowl. Add the courgettes, season with salt and freshly ground black pepper and toss to coat.

2. Heat a large griddle or frying pan over a high heat until hot. Add the courgettes and fry in a single layer until browned on both sides (you may need to do this in batches). Remove from the pan and set aside.

3. Add the peppers to the pan and fry for about 5 minutes until tinged brown but still with bite. Remove from the pan and set aside with the courgettes.

4. Bring a pan of water to the boil. Make a cross in the base of the tomatoes and place in the boiling water. Leave for 30 seconds. Drain and set aside until cool enough to handle. Remove the skins, then cut the tomatoes into slices.

5. Spread the lettuce leaves out on a serving plate and arrange the chargrilled vegetables, tomatoes and olives on top. Season well and scatter with half of the herbs.

6. Combine all the dressing ingredients in a jug and mix well. Add the remaining herbs to the dressing and season well.

7. Cut each piece of halloumi into two triangles. Heat the same griddle or frying pan over a high heat until very hot. Add the halloumi and fry for about 2 minutes on each side, until golden and soft in the middle.

8. Place the cheese on top of the vegetables and drizzle over the herb dressing to serve.

Asparagus and Fennel Salad with Tarragon Dressing

Vibrant and full of summer freshness, the tarragon dressing gives this simple salad a lift.

Serves 6

1 bulb fennel, trimmed

12 large asparagus spears, woody ends removed

2 Little Gem lettuces, shredded

25g (1oz) Parmesan shavings

For the tarragon dressing

2 tsp grainy mustard

1½ tbsp white wine vinegar

8 tbsp olive oil

1 tsp runny honey

1 tbsp freshly chopped tarragon

Mary's Tips

Can be assembled up to 6 hours ahead. Dress just before serving.

Not suitable for freezing.

1. Using a wide vegetable peeler, slice the fennel into strips.

2. Place the asparagus in a pan of boiling salted water and blanch for 2 minutes. Add the fennel strips and continue to boil both the vegetables for 1 minute. Drain and refresh the vegetables in cold water. Drain again and set aside to dry.

3. Meanwhile, make the dressing. Add all the ingredients to a bowl, season with salt and freshly ground black pepper and whisk to combine.

4. Scatter the shredded lettuce over the base of a platter or large bowl and arrange the fennel over the top. Criss-cross the asparagus spears and scatter the Parmesan shavings over the top. Pour over the dressing to serve.

Broccoli, Mango and Feta Salad

Fresh and super healthy, this is great for a crowd on a summer's evening.

Serves 6

75g (3oz) sourdough
   or ciabatta loaf, cut
   into 2cm (¾in) cubes
2 tbsp olive oil
200g (7oz) tenderstem
   broccoli, stems
   trimmed
2 Little Gem lettuces,
   torn into small pieces
150g (4½oz) mango,
   peeled and cut into
   2cm (¾in) cubes
   (prepared weight)
200g (7oz) feta
   cheese, crumbled
   into large pieces
6 slices Parma ham
4 tbsp pumpkin seeds

For the dressing
1 tbsp Dijon mustard
2 tbsp white wine
   vinegar
6 tbsp olive oil
1 tsp runny honey

Mary's Tips

*Can be assembled up to
5 hours ahead. Dress
just before serving.*

Not suitable for freezing.

1. Preheat the oven to 200°C/180°C Fan/Gas 6.

2. To make the croûtons, tip the sourdough or ciabatta cubes into a bowl and toss in the olive oil, then place on a baking sheet. Season with salt and freshly ground black pepper and bake in the preheated oven for about 10 minutes, until golden and crisp. Set aside.

3. Place the broccoli in a pan of boiling water and blanch for 3 minutes. Drain and refresh under cold water. Drain again and cut the stems into slices, leaving the tips.

4. Arrange the lettuce on a large platter and scatter the broccoli over the top. Scatter the mango, feta cheese and croûtons over the salad. Swirl the Parma ham slices and arrange on top, then sprinkle with the pumpkin seeds.

5. Place all the dressing ingredients in a small bowl, season with salt and freshly ground black pepper and whisk to combine. Pour over the salad just before serving.

Two Bean and Aubergine Salad with Garlic Balsamic Dressing

Bursting with texture and goodness, this salad will be perfect at any party or BBQ. It is important the beans and peas stay bright green for this salad, so cool with cold water after blanching; this stops them cooking and keeps them green.

Serves 6

2 aubergines, halved and thickly sliced

3 garlic cloves, unpeeled

4 tbsp olive oil

2 onions, sliced into wedges

150g (5oz) frozen or fresh soya beans

200g (7oz) French green beans, each sliced into 3

115g (4oz) frozen petits pois

200g (7oz) feta cheese, crumbled

For the garlic balsamic dressing

3 tbsp balsamic glaze

4 tbsp olive oil

2 tbsp freshly chopped thyme

Mary's Tips

Vegetables can be prepared up to 5 hours ahead. Dress just before serving.

Not suitable for freezing.

1. Preheat the oven to 220°C/200°C Fan/Gas 7. Line 2 large baking sheets with non-stick baking paper.

2. Arrange the aubergine slices in a single layer on one baking sheet and place the garlic cloves on top. Pour over half the olive oil and season with salt and freshly ground black pepper. Toss together. Put the onions and remaining oil on the second baking sheet and toss together. Place both sheets in the preheated oven and roast for about 20–35 minutes, until the onions and aubergines are tinged brown. Set aside to cool.

3. Bring a pan of water to the boil. Add the soya beans and bring back to the boil. Add the French beans and frozen petits pois and boil for 3 minutes. Drain and run under cold water until cold. Drain again and set aside to dry.

4. To make the dressing, squeeze the roasted garlic cloves from their skins into a large bowl and mash. Add the balsamic glaze and oil and mix well. Add all the vegetables to the bowl, along with the thyme and some seasoning. Toss everything together.

5. Tip the vegetables into a serving bowl and sprinkle with the feta to serve.

Lemon and Chive Coleslaw

Slaw is such a great dish to have in the fridge; it is so versatile and improves overnight. Pointed cabbage is sometimes called Hispi or sweetheart cabbage and has delicious tender leaves which hold their shape. It has much more flavour than a white cabbage, which would be more traditional for coleslaw. This very lemony slaw goes well with the Honey and Mustard Chicken on page 88.

Serves 6

1 pointed cabbage
2 carrots, peeled and coarsely grated
½ onion, finely sliced
Large bunch of chives, snipped

For the dressing
Juice of 1½ lemons
5 tbsp full-fat mayonnaise
100g (3½oz) full-fat crème fraîche

Mary's Tips

Can be made up to a day ahead.

Not suitable for freezing.

1. First make the dressing. Place the lemon juice, mayo and crème fraîche in a small bowl and mix together well. Season with salt and freshly ground black pepper.

2. Cut the cabbage into four wedges through the point, then cut out and discard the thick centre stem. Finely shred the remaining cabbage, using a sharp knife. Combine the cabbage, carrots, onion and chives together in a large bowl. Pour over the dressing and toss to coat.

3. Check the seasoning and serve.

Sweet Potato and Celeriac Slaw

**Using root vegetables in season gives a nice change from the classic.
This would be lovely with leftover roast beef (see page 110), or
served with the Venison and Bacon Burgers (see page 129).**

Serves 4–6

Finely grated zest
  and juice of 1 lime

1 tbsp white wine
  vinegar

Generous 1 tsp
  runny honey

2 tbsp grainy mustard

4 tbsp sunflower oil

225g (8oz) celeriac,
  peeled and sliced into
  very thin matchsticks
  (prepared weight)

2 large sticks celery,
  very thinly sliced

225g (8oz) sweet
  potato, peeled and
  sliced into very
  thin matchsticks
  (prepared weight)

½ red onion,
  thinly sliced

25g (1oz) dried
  cranberries,
  roughly chopped

Mary's Tips

*Salad will keep
for 2 days.*

Not suitable for freezing.

1. Mix the lime zest and juice, the vinegar, honey and mustard together in a large bowl. Gradually whisk in the oil.

2. Add the celeriac, celery, sweet potato and onion to the bowl and mix well to coat the vegetables in the dressing. Chill in the fridge until ready to serve.

3. Season with salt and freshly ground black pepper and scatter with the cranberries just before serving.

Brussels Sprout, Celeriac and Horseradish Slaw

Perfect for using any leftover raw sprouts at Christmas. This slaw goes well with cold meats and would be particularly good with Leek and Gruyère Tart (see page 162). I love sprouts but, if you're not sure, give this a go – it's surprisingly tasty!

Serves 6

200g (7oz) Brussels sprouts, finely shredded

8 tbsp full-fat mayonnaise

2 tbsp hot horseradish sauce

Juice of 1 lemon

150g (5oz) celeriac, peeled and coarsely grated (prepared weight)

2 thin sticks celery, thinly sliced

1 large carrot, coarsely grated

1 banana shallot, diced

Mary's Tips

Can be made up to 12 hours ahead.

Not suitable for freezing.

1. Remove and discard the darker outer leaves from the sprouts, then finely shred the remainder.

2. Spoon the mayonnaise, horseradish, lemon juice and plenty of salt and freshly ground black pepper into a large bowl. Mix together well.

3. Add the celeriac, celery, carrot, sprouts and shallot, and mix together to coat in the dressing.

4. Cover and leave to chill in the fridge until ready to serve.

Smashed New Potatoes with Garlic Herb Butter

An easy, rustic and tasty potato dish with our favourite flavours. We love to serve these potatoes with Sriracha Chicken Wings (see page 93).

Sriracha Chicken Wings (see page 93)

Serves 6

500g (1lb 2oz) baby new potatoes, halved if big

4 tbsp sunflower oil

25g (1oz) Parmesan, grated

For the garlic herb butter

55g (2oz) butter, melted

2 garlic cloves, finely grated

3 tbsp freshly chopped parsley

Mary's Tips

Garlic butter can be made up to 3 days ahead.

Not suitable for freezing.

1. Preheat the oven to 220°C/200°C Fan/Gas 7.

2. Parboil the potatoes in boiling salted water for about 10–12 minutes, or until nearly soft. Drain and set aside.

3. Pour the oil into a roasting tin and place in the preheated oven to get hot.

4. Tip the potatoes into the tin and toss in the hot oil. Using a potato masher, mash each potato once to crush them, then season with salt and freshly ground black pepper. Roast in the preheated oven for about 15–20 minutes until golden and crispy.

5. Meanwhile, make the garlic butter by mixing the ingredients together.

6. Remove the potatoes from the oven and pour the garlic butter over the top and toss to coat. Sprinkle over the cheese and return to the oven for a final 3–4 minutes. Serve straight from the oven.

Potato Wedges
with Bloody Mary Salt Mix

We were given the idea for this recipe on a girls' night out with lovely Alex Jones and our team after I visited *The One Show*. We promised we would make a recipe with this spiced dip and potato wedges, so here it is. Serve the wedges with the Sriracha Chicken Wings (see page 93) and you'll have a spicy dip for the wedges, too.

Serves 4–6

750g (1lb 10oz) old
   large potatoes,
   sliced into wedges,
   roughly the same
   size and shape
2 tbsp sunflower oil
1 tsp sun-dried
   tomato paste

For the salt mix
1 tsp ground coriander
1 tsp paprika
1 tsp celery salt
½ tsp ground ginger
Pinch of hot chilli
   powder
½ tsp caster sugar

For the dip
2 tsp sun-dried
   tomato paste
200ml tub full-fat
   crème fraîche

Mary's Tips

Best made and served.

Not suitable for freezing.

1. Preheat the oven to 220°C/200°C Fan/Gas 7. Line a large roasting tin with non-stick baking paper.

2. Arrange the potato wedges in the tin, pour over the oil and toss to coat. Add the sun-dried tomato paste and mix well to coat. Season well with salt and freshly ground black pepper. Roast in the preheated oven for 35 minutes, turning after about 15 minutes.

3. Meanwhile, measure the salt mix ingredients into a bowl and stir to combine.

4. Remove the potatoes from the oven and toss the potatoes in the salt mix.

5. To make the dip, mix the sun-dried tomato paste with the crème fraîche and serve in a bowl as a dip alongside the wedges.

Scruffy Potatoes

The perfect recipe where no style is needed. These potatoes benefit from being pushed around the pan and stirred erratically! It's all cooked on the hob, so they are an easy potato to make. Try these with the Chimichurri Pork on page 107.

Try these with the Chimichurri Pork on page 107.

Serves 4–6

3 tbsp sunflower oil

25g (1oz) butter

1 red onion,
   thinly sliced

500g (1lb 2oz) old
   potatoes, peeled and
   cut into thin (about
   0.5cm/¼in) slices
   (prepared weight)

2 garlic cloves,
   finely grated

2 tbsp freshly
   chopped parsley

Mary's Tips

*Can be made up to
3 hours ahead and
reheated to serve.*

Not suitable for freezing.

1. Heat the oil and butter in a very large frying pan over a medium–high heat. Add the onion and fry for 2 minutes. Add the potatoes and turn in the pan. Spread the potatoes out in an even layer and fry for 5 minutes. Cover with a lid and cook gently for 5–8 minutes.

2. Remove the lid, increase the heat, and fry, turning from time to time, for about 5 minutes, until the potatoes are tender and the onion is golden brown with some crispy edges. Add the garlic for the last few minutes.

3. Sprinkle with the parsley, season with salt and freshly ground black pepper and serve.

Super Crispy Roasted Celeriac

A great change from roast potatoes. Rolling the celeriac in semolina gives a crisp exterior. These would be lovely served with the Highland Beef Pie on page 116 or the venison fillet on page 130.

Serves 6

6 tbsp sunflower oil or goose fat

1kg (2lb 4oz) celeriac, peeled and chopped into 4cm (1½in) cubes (650g/1lb 7oz prepared weight)

3 tbsp semolina

Mary's Tips

Best made and served.

Not suitable for freezing.

1. Preheat the oven to 220°C/200°C Fan/Gas 7.

2. Measure the oil or goose fat into a large roasting tin. Place in the preheated oven to get hot for about 10 minutes.

3. Meanwhile, place the celeriac in a saucepan. Cover with cold salted water and bring up to the boil. Boil for about 4–5 minutes until just cooked. Drain well then tip back into the saucepan and remove from the heat. Sprinkle over the semolina and season with salt and freshly ground black pepper and toss together to coat.

4. Take the hot roasting tin out of the oven and add the celeriac. Turn once in the hot fat, making sure that the cubes are spaced out, then roast in the preheated oven for about 25 minutes.

5. Turn the celeriac and return to the oven to roast for a final 10–15 minutes until golden and crispy.

6. Serve piping hot.

Hot Beetroot and Horseradish

It's unusual to serve hot beetroot, but it really is delicious! Make sure to use a coarse grater for the beetroot, though. If you use a fine grater, it will become a mush. The horseradish complements the earthy flavour of the beetroot and is my absolute favourite veg. Beetroot is one of the easiest vegetables to grow, too. This would be lovely served with the Roast Rib of Beef with Parsnips and Carrots on page 110 or the Highland Beef Pie on page 116.

Serves 4–6

4 tbsp pouring double cream

2 heaped tbsp hot horseradish sauce

500g (1lb 2oz) cooked beetroot, peeled and coarsely grated

Mary's Tips

Hot horseradish from a jar is ideal but if you have fresh, grate it into the cream and cook it until soft before adding the beetroot.

Not suitable for freezing.

1. Place the cream and horseradish in a large frying pan and bring up to the boil. Add the beetroot and stir over the heat for a few minutes until hot.

2. Season well with salt and freshly ground black pepper and serve in a warmed dish.

Aromatic Basmati Nut Rice

Wonderful flavours and perfect to serve with the Cauliflower and Sweet Potato Curry on page 154 or the Super Easy Mango Chicken on page 84.

Wonderful flavours and perfect to serve with the Cauliflower and Sweet Potato Curry on page 154 or the Super Easy Mango Chicken on page 84.

Serves 4–6

150g (5oz) basmati rice

1 tbsp sunflower oil

1 onion, thinly sliced

2 garlic cloves, finely grated

3 cardamon pods, crushed

350ml (12fl oz) vegetable or chicken stock

Good grating of nutmeg

4 lime leaves

2 bay leaves

½ lime

Small bunch of coriander, leaves roughly chopped

1 tbsp flaked almonds, toasted

1 tbsp pistachios, chopped

Mary's Tips

Can be made up to 6 hours ahead. Reheat in an oven at a very low temperature, in a dish with buttered paper on top.

Not suitable for freezing.

1. Wash the rice, then drain and set aside.

2. Heat the oil in a saucepan with a lid over a high heat. Add the onion and cook for 3 minutes. Add the garlic and crushed cardamon pods and fry for 1 minute. Stir in the rice and pour in the stock. Add the nutmeg, lime and bay leaves, and the half lime. Cover with a lid, reduce the heat and simmer for about 15 minutes, until all the liquid has absorbed.

3. Remove the lid and season with salt and freshly ground black pepper. Stir in the coriander and nuts, and serve in an open dish.

Chargrilled Pointed Cabbage with Tomato Dressing

This is quite a different dish to serve as a side; try it with the Sriracha Chicken Wings on page 93 or the Chimichurri Pork on page 107. The tomato dressing would be a lovely alternative to the chimichurri. I also enjoy it on its own.

Serves 4

1 large pointed cabbage
1 tbsp olive oil

For the dressing
2 tsp sun-dried tomato paste
2 tsp white wine vinegar
3 tbsp olive oil
½ small garlic clove, finely grated
A few drops of sriracha sauce

Mary's Tips

Cabbage can be blanched up to 2 hours ahead. Fry or griddle to serve.

Not suitable for freezing.

1. Measure all the dressing ingredients together in a small jug and season well with salt and freshly ground black pepper.

2. Remove any hard outer leaves from the cabbage and lightly trim the base. Slice the cabbage into four quarters, keeping the heart attached.

3. Bring a pan of salted water to the boil. Add the cabbage quarters and blanch for 1–1½ minutes, depending on the size. Drain and refresh under cold water. Drain again and dry well.

4. When ready to serve, heat a large frying pan or griddle over a high heat until very hot. Brush the cabbage with the oil and season well. Fry the wedges for about 1½ minutes or until charred and dark brown. Turn the cabbage and brown on the other sides.

5. Remove from the pan or griddle and place on a hot serving plate. Pour over the dressing and serve.

Little Yorkshire Puddings

A classic with roast beef (see page 110), the secret is to get the oil very hot before adding the batter, and slide the tray into the middle of the oven – not too near the top or they will struggle to rise. Made in a bun tin, these are smaller than the usual large puddings most restaurants serve.

Makes 12

100g (3¾oz) plain flour
¼ tsp salt
3 eggs
225ml (8fl oz) milk
Sunflower oil, goose
  or duck fat or
  beef dripping

Mary's Tips

The puddings can be made completely ahead and reheated. Place them back in the tins in a hot oven for about 8 minutes. The batter can be made up to 2 hours ahead.

Freeze well cooked.

1. Preheat the oven to 220°C/200°C Fan/Gas 7. You will need a 12-hole deep bun tin.

2. Measure the flour and salt into a bowl and make a well in the centre. Add the eggs and a little milk. Whisk until smooth, then gradually add the remaining milk. These can be made by hand but are best made with an electric whisk until the bubbles burst on the surface. Pour the batter into a jug.

3. Measure a dessertspoon of oil into each hole of the 12-hole tin. Transfer to the preheated oven for about 5–10 minutes, depending on the thickness of the tins, until the oil is piping hot.

4. Carefully remove the tin from the oven and pour in the batter straight away, dividing it equally between the holes. Return to the oven and cook for about 20–25 minutes until golden brown and well risen.

5. Lift out of the tins and serve immediately.

French Peas

This is a classic French dish, which sounds a little odd but is delicious. Sometimes we add crispy bacon pieces, too. A very soft lettuce would have been used traditionally for this dish, but I like Little Gem, as they keep some of their crispness. Serve these with pan-fried mackerel (see page 70) or sausages (see page 108).

Serves 4

60g (2¼oz) butter, at room temperature

2 Little Gem lettuces, leaves separated

450g (1lb) frozen peas

4 small shallots, quartered

10 mint leaves

75ml (2½fl oz) white wine

Mary's Tips

Best made and served.

Not suitable for freezing.

1. Melt half the butter in a wide-based saucepan. Use the outer leaves of the lettuces to line the pan.

2. Add the peas and shallot wedges to the pan. Cube the rest of the butter and dot over the top. Season well with salt and freshly ground pepper, then sprinkle in the mint and pour in the wine. Lay the remaining lettuce leaves over the peas so they are encased top and bottom. Cover with a lid and simmer gently for about 20–25 minutes.

3. Remove the lid, stir and check the seasoning.

4. Spoon into a warm dish to serve.

Hasselback Squash
with Honey and Ginger

The word Hasselback originates from the 1940s and a chef in a Swedish restaurant of that name, who served Hasselback potatoes. It is super easy to use this technique for squash. Serve them in two halves. It is a side dish but if you wish to make it more of a meal add some crumbled feta cheese and pine nuts just before serving.

Serves 6

1 medium butternut
  squash (about
  1kg/2lb 4oz)
Large bunch of thyme
2 tbsp sunflower oil
2 tbsp runny honey
5cm (2in) piece of fresh
  root ginger, grated
1 tbsp sea salt flakes
2 tbsp freshly
  chopped parsley

Mary's Tips

*Squash can be prepared
up to 4 hours ahead.
Pour over the glaze
just before roasting.*

Not suitable for freezing.

1. Preheat the oven to 200°C/180°C Fan/Gas 6. Line a shallow roasting tin with non-stick baking paper.

2. Cut the squash in half lengthways through the middle of the stem. Scoop out the seeds and discard. Using a small sharp knife, carefully cut the skin from the flesh, keeping the flesh in one piece.

3. Split the bunch of thyme into two piles and place on the roasting tin. Sit each squash half, cut-side down, on top of the thyme (this will give a thyme flavour to the flesh of the squash). Using a small sharp knife, carefully cut the flesh horizontally, 0.5cm (¼in) apart, two-thirds of the way through the squash, to give slashes.

4. Mix the oil, honey and ginger together in a small bowl. Spoon over the squash and spread to coat. Season with salt and freshly ground black pepper and roast in the preheated oven for about 45–55 minutes, until slightly charred, golden and tender. Baste any juices over the squash during cooking.

5. Serve piping hot sprinkled with the sea salt flakes and parsley.

Bay and Lemon Brown Rice

Fragrant rice, perfect to serve with Rugby Lamb (see page 125).

Fragrant rice, perfect to serve with Rugby Lamb (see page 125).

Serves 4–6

200g (7oz) long grain brown rice

Knob of butter

2 garlic cloves, finely grated

500ml (18fl oz) vegetable stock

Finely grated zest of 1 lemon

4 bay leaves

Mary's Tips

Can be made up to 6 hours ahead. Reheat in an oven at a very low temperature, in a dish with buttered paper on top.

Not suitable for freezing.

1. Wash the rice, then drain and set aside.

2. Heat the butter in a saucepan with a lid over a high heat. Add the garlic and fry for 1 minute. Stir in the rice to coat in the garlic butter and fry for 1 minute.

3. Add the stock, lemon zest and bay leaves to the pan and bring up to a boil. Cover with a lid, reduce the heat and simmer gently for about 25 minutes, until the stock has been absorbed and the rice is cooked.

Puddings

Toffee Fudge Tart

The toffee is indulgent and sweet but the thin layer of sour cream cuts through the sweetness. It is important to chill this well before cutting to prevent the filling from being too soft.

For the base

150g (5oz) digestive biscuits (about 10), crushed

75g (3oz) butter, melted

For the toffee filling

75g (3oz) butter

75g (3oz) light muscovado sugar

1 × 397g tin full-fat condensed milk

1 tsp vanilla extract

For the topping

150ml (¼ pint) sour cream

165g (5½oz) full-fat cream cheese

4 pieces of fudge, grated

You will need a 20cm (8in) round loose-bottomed sandwich tin.

Mary's Tips

Make up to a day ahead.

Freezes well.

1. To make the base, measure the biscuits and butter into a bowl and mix to combine. Spoon into the base of the tin and press down with the back of a spoon until level. Chill in the fridge for 15 minutes.

2. To make the toffee filling, place the butter and sugar in a small non-stick saucepan and stir over a low heat until melted. Add the condensed milk and bring to the boil, stirring all the time, and cook for about 2–3 minutes, until golden, thick and toffee-coloured. Do not over-boil or it will become grainy. Add the vanilla and stir, then pour into the tin on top of the biscuit crust. Chill in the fridge for about an hour until set.

3. Mix the sour cream and the cream cheese in a bowl and stir until smooth. Spread over the top of the toffee filling, then decorate with the grated fudge. Chill in the fridge overnight.

4. Cut into wedges to serve.

Tarte au Citron

A wonderful classic lemon tart with crisp shortcrust pastry.

Serves 10

For the shortcrust pastry
225g (8oz) plain flour
115g (4oz) butter, cubed
2 tbsp icing sugar
1 large egg, beaten

For the filling
9 large eggs, beaten
300ml (½ pint) pouring double cream
300g (10½oz) caster sugar
Zest and juice of 6 large lemons

Mary's Tips

Can be made up to a day ahead.

Freezes well.

1. You will need a 28cm (11in) deep, fluted, loose-bottomed tart tin.

2. To make the pastry, measure the flour, butter and icing sugar into a food processor. Whiz until breadcrumb stage. Add the egg and 1 tablespoon water and whiz again until the pastry comes together.

3. Roll out the pastry on a lightly floured work surface and use to line the tart tin. Prick the base with a fork and chill in the fridge for 30 minutes.

4. Preheat the oven to 200°C/180°C Fan/Gas 6.

5. To bake blind, line the pastry with non-stick baking paper and baking beans and blind bake the pastry case in the preheated oven for about 15 minutes. Remove the paper and beans and bake for another 5 minutes, until golden and crisp.

6. Meanwhile, whisk the eggs, cream and sugar together in a bowl for a few minutes until combined. Add the lemon zest and juice and whisk well. Pour into a large jug.

7. Reduce the oven temperature to 140°C/120°C Fan/Gas 1. Pull the oven shelf and tart case halfway out of the oven. Pour the mixture into the case and carefully push the shelf back into place. Bake for about 35 minutes until set with a slight wobble in the centre. Leave to cool.

8. Serve warm with cream.

Chocolate Truffle Tart

Delicious, rich and very naughty. Be sure to use chocolate that has around 40% cocoa solids to ensure it has a smooth texture and sets perfectly. The base of the tart is like rocky road without the marshmallows, so it is very indulgent!

Serves 10

For the base
100g (3½oz) butter

135g (4¾oz) Bournville chocolate, broken into pieces

2½ tbsp golden syrup

165g (5½oz) Nice biscuits, broken into 5mm (¼in) pieces

For the chocolate mousse filling
180g (6¼oz) Bournville chocolate, broken into pieces

100g (3½oz) caster sugar

4 tbsp Baileys cream liqueur

300ml (½ pint) pouring double cream

For the decoration
12 truffle chocolates

Icing sugar, to dust

Mary's Tips

Can be made up to a day ahead.

Freezes well.

1. Line the base of a 23cm (9in) springform tin with non-stick baking paper. (Do not grease the base.)

2. To make the base, measure the butter, chocolate and golden syrup into a bowl. Heat gently over a pan of simmering water, making sure the base of the bowl doesn't touch the water, until melted, stirring until smooth.

3. Add the biscuit pieces to the chocolate mixture and stir to coat. Spoon into the base of the tin and press down with the back of a spoon until level. Chill in the fridge for 30 minutes until firm.

4. Release the spring sides and remove the firm biscuit base from the tin. Discard the baking paper underneath, then return the biscuit to the tin base and resecure the springform sides. This is a foolproof way to ensure the base does not stick.

5. To make the filling, place the chocolate in a food processor. Whiz until you have a fine powder. Measure the caster sugar into a saucepan with 6 tablespoons of water. Dissolve over a low heat until clear. Boil for 1 minute. Pour the sugar syrup into the food processor and whiz until the chocolate has melted. Add the Baileys and whiz again.

6. Whisk the cream in a large bowl until medium–firm peaks. Pour the chocolate mixture into the cream and carefully fold together until smooth. Spoon onto the biscuit base and chill in the fridge overnight.

7. To serve, arrange the chocolate truffles around the edge of the tart and dust lightly with icing sugar. Make sure you serve

straight from the fridge. Run a hot palette knife around the edge of the mousse and release the sides of the tin. Slide a palette knife under the base and transfer the tart to a serving plate.

8. Cut into wedges to serve, with extra pouring cream, if liked.

Pecan and Treacle Tart

A classic for so many reasons – crisp, short pastry and a filling full of flavour. A warming favourite for all the family.

Serves 6

500g (1lb 2oz)
   golden syrup
Zest and juice of
   1 large lemon
175g (6oz) white
   breadcrumbs (made
   from a loaf that is
   a few days old)
55g (2oz) pecan nuts

For the pastry
175g (6oz) plain flour
75g (3oz) butter, cubed
2 tbsp icing sugar
1 egg, beaten

**You will need a
20cm (8in) deep,
loose-bottomed,
fluted tart tin.**

Mary's Tips

*Can be made up to a day
ahead and reheated.*

Freezes well.

1. To make the pastry, measure the flour, butter and icing sugar into a food processor. Whiz until breadcrumb stage. Add the egg and whiz until the dough comes together. Tip out onto a lightly floured work surface and roll until slightly larger than the tart tin. Use to line the tin, then prick the pastry with a fork and place in the fridge to chill for 30 minutes.

2. Preheat the oven to 200°C/180°C Fan/Gas 6.

3. To bake blind, cover the pastry with non-stick baking paper and tip in some baking beans. Bake blind in the preheated oven for 15 minutes. Remove the beans and the paper and bake for another 5 minutes, until the pastry is golden and crisp.

4. Reduce the oven temperature to 180°C/160°C Fan/Gas 4.

5. Measure the syrup into a saucepan and place over a low heat. Warm gently until runny. Add the lemon zest and juice, then mix in the breadcrumbs. Stir well, remove from the heat and set aside for 5 minutes.

6. Pour the filling into the tart case, arrange the pecan nuts on top and bake for about 30–40 minutes until pale golden and set, but with a slight wobble in the middle.

7. Leave to cool slightly before slicing into wedges. Serve warm with cream.

Starlight Fruits

A wonderful combination of oranges and nectarines. Very simple but lovely to have as an alternative to a rich pudding. Peaches or apricots, when in season, would be lovely, too.

Serves 4–6

6 large oranges
200ml (⅓ pint)
    white wine
200ml (⅓ pint) water
115g (4oz) caster sugar
4 nectarines, cut
    into thin wedges

Mary's Tips

*Can be made up to
8 hours ahead.*

Not suitable for freezing.

1. Segment the oranges by removing the skin and any pith with a small knife, then carefully cutting either side of the orange segments to remove them.

2. Measure the wine, water and caster sugar into a large saucepan. Stir gently over a low heat until the sugar has dissolved, then boil the syrup for 3 minutes until reduced.

3. Add the nectarines to the pan and simmer for about 5 minutes over a low heat. Add the oranges and simmer for about 2 minutes, or until the nectarines are soft, but still holding their shape. Spoon the fruits into a serving bowl and set aside.

4. Continue to reduce the syrup until halved, then set aside to cool.

5. Pour the syrup over the fruits and chill in the fridge until ready to serve.

Honeydew Fruit Salad

**So fresh and light as a dessert, but also lovely for breakfast.
I am always thinking of new fruit combinations and like to offer a fruit
salad as an option. Best serve chilled. Lychees are sometimes difficult to
find in supermarkets, but are always available in Asian supermarkets.**

Serves 6

1 just-ripe honeydew
melon, peeled,
deseeded and
flesh cut into 2cm
(¾in) chunks

4 kiwis, peeled,
quartered and each
piece halved

½ bunch of green
grapes, halved

1 × 425g tin lychees
in syrup

2 tbsp freshly
chopped mint

4 tbsp elderflower
cordial

Mary's Tips

*Can be made up to
6 hours ahead and
kept in the fridge.*

*You can use 6 fresh
lychees instead of
the tinned lychees, if
available. Add 100ml
(3½fl oz) water to the
elderflower cordial in
place of the syrup.*

1. Place the melon, kiwis and grapes in a bowl.

2. Drain the lychees, reserving 100ml (3½fl oz) of the syrup, and place them in the bowl with the other fruit. Sprinkle over the mint.

3. Mix the reserved lychee syrup with the cordial in a small jug. Pour over the fruit and stir. Chill in the fridge until ready to serve.

Spiced Poached Pears
with Blackberry Compote

A refreshingly simple compote with a hint of spice to serve as a pudding. Perfect for breakfast, too, with a dollop of natural yoghurt. Adding the spices to the warm liquid will help the flavours infuse deeply.

Serves 4–6

600ml (1 pint)
  apple juice
100g (3½oz)
  caster sugar
Peeled zest of 1 lemon
2 cinnamon sticks
5 star anise
4–6 ripe but firm
  pears, peeled,
  halved and cored
2 tsp cornflour
225g (8oz) blackberries

Mary's Tips

*Can be made up to
6 hours ahead.*

Not suitable for freezing.

1. Measure the apple juice, caster sugar and 600ml (1 pint) water into a saucepan. Bring up to the boil, stirring, until the sugar has dissolved and the liquid is clear. Add the lemon zest, cinnamon and star anise to the warm liquid.

2. Add the pears to the poaching liquid and simmer for 15 minutes, until tender. Remove the pears from the syrup and place in a serving bowl.

3. Reduce the poaching liquid by a third until syrupy.

4. Mix the cornflour with 2 tablespoons of cold water in a cup, then add a little of the hot syrup to the cornflour and stir well. Return the mixture to the pan, bring to the boil, stirring, until thickened slightly. Pour over the pears and set aside to cool.

5. Once cold, stir in the blackberries.

6. Remove the whole spices and serve cold with crème fraîche or Greek yoghurt.

Caramelised Pear Brûlée

**In all my books I like to add a pud in a little pot, ramekin or glass –
something you can make ahead, which puts your mind at rest that
one pudding at least is done! We prefer full-fat yoghurt and crème
fraîche, but you can use the lighter versions, if preferred.**

Serves 6–8

6 ripe conference pears
Large knob of butter
90g (3½oz) light
  muscovado sugar
200g (7oz) full-fat
  Greek yoghurt
200g (7oz) full-fat
  crème fraîche

Mary's Tips

*Can be made up to
6 hours ahead.*

Not suitable for freezing.

1. Peel the pears using a potato peeler. Remove the stalks, slice
   each pear in half and scoop out the core. Slice the flesh into
   small chunks.

2. Melt the butter in a frying pan over a medium heat. Add
   3 tablespoons of the sugar and stir until dissolved. Add the
   pears and stir over the heat until caramelised, golden and
   sticky. Remove from the heat and set aside to cool. Divide
   between six small glass pots or glasses.

3. Mix the yoghurt and crème fraîche together in a bowl.
   Spoon the mixture on top of the pears and level the surface.

4. Sprinkle the remaining sugar over the puddings and chill
   until ready to serve.

Cranachan Pavlova Wreath

This pavlova with a Scottish twist is perfect for the festive period to be enjoyed by all. Cranachan is a traditional Scottish dessert of oats, fruit and cream.

Serves 8–10

Knob of butter

25g (1oz) light muscovado sugar

75g (3oz) old-fashioned porridge oats

600ml (1 pint) double cream

2 tbsp whisky

450g (1lb) raspberries

200g (7oz) blueberries

55g (2oz) pomegranate seeds

Small sprigs of rosemary

Icing sugar, to dust

For the meringue

6 large egg whites

350g (12oz) caster sugar

1 tsp white wine vinegar

1 tsp cornflour

Mary's Tips

Can be made up to a week ahead. Fill with cream and fruits up to 4 hours ahead.

Pavlova freezes well in a box as it is fragile.

1. Preheat the oven to 160°C/140°C Fan/Gas 3. Line a large baking sheet with non-stick baking paper and draw a 30cm (12in) circle in the middle of the paper. Draw a 15cm (6in) circle in the centre of the larger circle to make a ring.

2. To make the meringue, place the egg whites in a clean mixing bowl and whisk with an electric whisk until light and fluffy. Gradually add the caster sugar, a little at a time, whisking on maximum speed, until stiff and glossy. Mix the vinegar and cornflour in a small cup until smooth, then stir into the meringue.

3. Spoon the meringue onto the ring drawn on the baking paper. Using a large spoon, make a shallow trench ring in the centre of the meringue for the cream and fruit. Transfer to the oven and immediately reduce the temperature to 140°C/120°C Fan/Gas 1. Bake for 1 hour–1 hour 15 minutes, until the outside of the meringue is hard but still white. Turn the oven off and leave the meringue inside for an hour or overnight to cool and dry.

4. Melt the butter in a small frying pan over a medium heat. Add the light muscovado sugar and oats and fry until the oats are lightly golden brown and the sugar has melted and is coating the oats. Remove from the heat and set aside to cool.

5. To assemble the pavlova, whip the cream until soft peaks, then stir in the whisky. Add two-thirds of the oats and half the raspberries to the cream and mix well. Spoon this cream mixture into the trench in the meringue. Arrange the remaining raspberries, blueberries and pomegranate seeds on top and decorate with a few rosemary sprigs, to look like small Christmas trees. Sprinkle with the remaining oats.

6. Dust with icing sugar and cut into wedges to serve.

Glazed Strawberry Ice Cream

Ice cream is always popular and great to have at the ready in case friends pop in without notice. If you serve it with fresh strawberries and a piece of shortbread biscuit, it's a quick and easy pud.

Serves 6–8

115g (4oz) caster sugar
500g (1lb 2oz)
   strawberries, sliced
Juice of 1 small lemon
4 eggs, separated
300ml (½ pint) pouring
   double cream,
   whisked to soft peaks
25g (1oz) white
   chocolate, shavings

Mary's Tips

*Can be made up to
a month ahead.*

1. Measure 25g (1oz) of the caster sugar into a bowl. Add the strawberries and stir to coat. Set aside for 30 minutes.

2. Put the glazed strawberries into a food processor with any liquid from the bowl. Blend to a smooth purée. Add the lemon juice.

3. Put the egg whites into a bowl and whisk with an electric mixer until cloud-like. Add a teaspoon of the remaining caster sugar and whisk again. Continue to add the sugar a teaspoon at a time, whisking all the time on full speed, until all the remaining sugar has been incorporated and you have a glossy meringue.

4. Beat the yolks in a small bowl using a fork.

5. Whisk the cream in a large bowl to soft peaks with an electric whisk.

6. Fold the meringue and strawberry purée into the cream until you have a smooth pink mixture. Fold in the yolks, being careful not to lose any air from the egg whites.

7. Spoon into a container and freeze for a minimum of 6 hours or overnight. Remove from the freezer about 10 minutes before serving to soften.

8. Serve with a small bowl of white chocolate shavings to sprinkle over the ice cream.

Baileys Ice Cream

**The most luxurious ice cream! This is boozy and creamy, and so good
with the Upside-down Apricot and Cointreau Pudding on page 240.**

Makes 600ml
(1 pint)

4 eggs, separated
115g (4oz) caster sugar
250g (9oz) full-fat
   mascarpone
1 tsp vanilla extract
6 tbsp Baileys

Mary's Tips

*Remove from the freezer
5 minutes before serving
so it is easier to scoop.*

*Can be frozen
for a month.*

1. Place the egg whites in a large bowl and whisk using an
   electric whisk until they are like clouds. Add the caster
   sugar, a teaspoon at a time, whisking all the time on full
   speed, until it is a thick, glossy meringue.

2. Place the mascarpone in another bowl and beat to loosen.
   Add the egg yolks, vanilla and Baileys and whisk until
   smooth. Whisk in a few tablespoons of the meringue,
   then gently fold in the remaining meringue, until well
   incorporated.

3. Spoon into a container and place in the freezer overnight.

Strawberry and Passionfruit Shortbread Dessert

A lovely, fresh pud. If you can't find passionfruit curd, use lemon curd instead; it's just as delicious. The shortbread base gives a lovely crisp change to pastry.

Serves 6

For the shortbread base
115g (4oz) plain flour
55g (2oz) semolina
55g (2oz) caster sugar
115g (4oz) butter

For the topping
3 tbsp passionfruit curd
200g (7oz) mascarpone cheese
150ml (¼ pint) pouring double cream
3 passionfruit
350g (12oz) strawberries, sliced
2 tbsp redcurrant jelly

Mary's Tips

The shortbread base can be made a day ahead. Assemble up to 4 hours ahead.

Shortbread base freezes well.

1. To make the shortbread base, measure the plain flour, semolina, caster sugar and butter into a food processor and whiz until the mixture comes together.

2. Tip the dough out onto some non-stick baking paper and roll out to a round circle with a diameter about 20cm (8in). Flute the edges and prick the surface with a fork. Slide the dough and the paper onto a baking sheet and chill in the fridge for about 30 minutes until cold.

3. Preheat the oven to 160°C/140°C Fan/Gas 3.

4. Bake the shortbread in the preheated oven for about 35–40 minutes, until pale golden and firm in the middle. Turn off the oven and leave the shortbread inside for a further 15 minutes. Set aside to cool.

5. When the shortbread is completely cold, place it on a large flat serving plate. Spread with the passionfruit curd.

6. Measure the mascarpone and cream into a bowl. Whisk gently for a couple of minutes, until thickened, then stir in the pulp from 2 passionfruit. Spread this cream mixture over the passionfruit curd. Arrange the strawberries on top in a pretty pattern, then spoon over the remaining passionfruit pulp.

7. To glaze, melt the redcurrant jelly with 2 teaspoons of water in a small pan over a gentle heat. Brush the glaze over the strawberries just before serving.

White Chocolate Roulade

We have all been making dark chocolate roulade for years. Well, here is a delicious white chocolate one! White chocolate can be temperamental, so melt it gently and do not overheat, otherwise the chocolate will sink to the bottom of the sponge or be lumpy and split.

Serves 6–8

For the roulade
175g (6oz) Continental white chocolate, broken into pieces
6 large eggs, separated
175g (6oz) caster sugar
1 tsp vanilla extract
55g (2oz) plain flour
Icing sugar, to dust

For the filling
300ml (½ pint) double cream
1 tsp vanilla extract
225g (8oz) raspberries

To decorate
75g (3oz) Continental white chocolate, broken into pieces

Mary's Tips

Can be made and assembled up to 4 hours ahead.

Freezes well filled.

1. Preheat the oven to 180°C/160°C Fan/Gas 4. Grease and line a 33 × 23cm (13 × 9in) Swiss roll tin with non-stick baking paper.

2. To make the roulade, place the chocolate in a bowl over a pan of simmering water, making sure the base of the bowl doesn't touch the water. Melt until runny, then leave to cool slightly.

3. Meanwhile, whisk the egg whites using an electric whisk on full speed, until stiff but not dry. In a separate bowl, whisk the egg yolks and caster sugar using an electric whisk, until thick ribbon stage and pale in colour.

4. Stir the vanilla and melted chocolate into the egg yolk mixture. Add 1 tablespoon of the egg whites to the yolks and stir to slacken the mixture slightly. Carefully fold in the remaining whites until combined. Sift the flour into the bowl and gently fold until incorporated (be careful not to knock out the air). Pour into the prepared tin and level the surface. Bake in the preheated oven for about 20–25 minutes, until pale golden and firm in the centre. Leave to cool. To make the filling, whip the cream until thick, then stir in the vanilla and raspberries.

5. Dust a large piece of non-stick baking paper with icing sugar, then flip the roulade onto it. Carefully remove the tin and paper from the base. Score a line 2cm (¼in) in from one long edge. Spread the filling over the surface of the roulade. Starting with the scored edge, roll the roulade up tightly using the paper to help. Place on a serving plate.

6. To decorate, melt the white chocolate as above, then drizzle over the roulade in a zig-zag pattern. Finally, dust with icing sugar and slice into thick slices to serve.

Party Cheesecake
with Mango and Passionfruit Salsa

A super way of feeding a crowd. Made in a traybake tin, it is very easy to cut into small squares, which is the perfect amount for a gathering or party.

Cuts into
16 pieces

For the base
100g (3½oz) butter, melted
200g (7oz) Digestive
  biscuits, finely crushed

For the filling
700g (1lb 9oz) full-
  fat cream cheese
125g (4½oz) caster sugar
1 tbsp plain flour
2 tsp vanilla extract
Finely grated zest
  of ½ lemon
1 tsp fresh lemon juice
2 eggs, beaten
150g (5oz) sour cream

**For the mango and
passionfruit salsa**
2 passionfruit
350g (12oz) mango,
  peeled and diced
  (prepared weight)
Juice of ½ lime
2 tbsp icing sugar

Mary's Tips

*Can be made up to a day
ahead. Spoon the salsa
over the top to serve.*

Cheesecake freezes well.

1. Preheat the oven to 160°C/140°C Fan/Gas 3. Grease and line a 30 × 23cm (12 × 9in) traybake tin with non-stick baking paper.

2. To make the biscuit base, combine the melted butter with the crushed biscuits and mix well. Spoon into the base of the tin and press down with the back of a spoon until level. Leave to chill in the fridge.

3. Meanwhile, place the cream cheese in a large bowl. Whisk on a gentle speed using an electric whisk. Add the caster sugar, plain flour, vanilla extract, lemon zest and juice, and whisk again. Slowly whisk in the eggs and sour cream.

4. Spoon into the tin and level the top. Bake in the preheated oven for about 40 minutes, then turn the oven off and leave it there for 2 hours until completely set. Once cool, leave to chill in the fridge overnight.

5. To make the salsa, cut the passionfruit in half and scoop out the pulp and seeds. Combine all the salsa ingredients in a bowl and mix together.

6. When ready to serve, trim the edges of the cheesecake to neaten, then cut the cheesecake into 16 rectangles and spoon the salsa on top. Serve on a platter.

Black Forest Trifle

Black forest gateau was a classic in the 80s. I have made so many in my time. Flavour combinations from the past are often so good they deserve a reboot! Cherry compote comes in a jar and you can find it in the jam section at supermarkets. If you do not have a bottle of kirsch, use brandy. Some bourbon biscuits soften more quickly than others, so keep checking; they want to be just soft with a little texture, not mushy.

Serves 6–8

250g (9oz) mascarpone

4 tbsp icing sugar

300ml (½ pint) pouring double cream

400g (14oz) cherry compote

25 chocolate bourbon biscuits

8 tbsp kirsch

25g (1oz) plain chocolate, grated

You will need a 1.4-litre (2½-pint) trifle dish.

Mary's Tips

Can be made up to 6 hours ahead.

Not suitable for freezing.

1. Measure the mascarpone and icing sugar into a bowl. Beat together with a spatula to loosen the mascarpone. Add the cream and gently whisk until soft peaks. (Be careful not to over-whisk or it will be too thick.)

2. Spoon half the compote into the base of the trifle dish. Place half the bourbon biscuits on top in a single layer and press down. Sprinkle over half the kirsch to soak into the biscuits. Spread half of the cream mixture on top. Repeat with the remaining compote, biscuits and kirsch, and finish with a layer of the cream mixture.

3. Sprinkle with the grated chocolate and chill in the fridge for 2–4 hours.

Upside-down Apricot and Cointreau Pudding

Great for family gatherings, serve this with crème fraîche for a wonderful treat. The apricot season is very short in the UK, so we use tinned for this recipe, but destoned fresh apricots would be delicious, too. The topping does not work as well in a non-stick pan, so it is best to use stainless-steel.

Serves 6–8

Butter, melted, or
  sunflower oil
2 × 400g tins apricot
  halves in syrup,
  drained well and
  lightly dried on
  kitchen paper

For the topping
125g (4½oz)
  granulated sugar
75g (3oz) butter
2 tbsp Cointreau

For the sponge
115g (4oz) self-
  raising flour
115g (4oz) baking
  spread, straight
  from the fridge
115g (4oz) caster sugar
2 eggs
Finely grated zest of
  1 small orange
1 tbsp Cointreau

Mary's Tips

*Can be made up to
12 hours ahead and
gently warmed to serve.*

Freezes well.

1. Preheat the oven to 180°C/160°C Fan/Gas 4. You will need a deep, fixed-base 20cm (8in) cake tin. (There's no need to line the base.)

2. To make the topping, measure the granulated sugar and 4 tablespoons of water into a stainless-steel pan. Stir over a medium heat until the sugar has dissolved. Stop stirring and bring up to the boil. Boil until the sugar turns a deep caramel colour. Quickly remove from the heat and add knobs of the butter and the Cointreau. Stir, then pour into the base of the cake tin.

3. Brush the sides of the tin with the melted butter or oil. Arrange the apricot halves on top of the caramel, whichever way up you prefer. Place any extra apricots in a neat layer over the top.

4. Measure the sponge ingredients into a bowl. Whisk for 1½–2 minutes with an electric whisk, until light and fluffy. Spoon on top of the apricots and level the surface. Bake in the preheated oven for about 50–55 minutes, until lightly golden and the sponge is coming away from the sides of the tin.

5. Leave to stand for about 30 minutes, then loosen the sides and put a plate on top. Carefully turn the cake upside down and remove the tin.

6. Spoon any loose caramel sauce over the top and serve warm in wedges.

Foolproof Floating Islands

The classic way to make the French *îles flottantes* or floating islands is to poach the meringue, but I cook them gently in the oven on top of the custard and this makes for a quick and smart pud.

Serves 6–8

Butter, for greasing
600ml (1 pint)
   full-fat milk
3 eggs, separated
200g (7oz) caster sugar
1 rounded tbsp
   cornflour
2 tsp vanilla extract

For the caramel
25g (1oz) caster sugar

Mary's Tips

Best made and served.

Not suitable for freezing.

1. Preheat the oven to 140°C/120°C Fan/Gas 1. Grease a 26cm (10in) shallow ovenproof dish with butter.

2. To make the custard, pour the milk into a saucepan and heat until just below boiling point. Place the egg yolks in a bowl with 2 tablespoons of the caster sugar, the cornflour and vanilla extract. Mix well. Pour in the hot milk and whisk. Clean the saucepan, then pour the mixture through a sieve into the saucepan. Stir over a medium heat until the custard has thickened throughout. Pour into the prepared dish.

3. Tip the egg whites into a clean bowl or free-standing mixer and whisk on full speed until stiff. Add the remaining caster sugar a teaspoon at a time, while whisking on full speed, until thick and glossy. Make 8 quenelles of the meringue and place them in a single layer on top of the custard.

4. Carefully slide the dish into the preheated oven for about 15–20 minutes until the meringues have set and are no longer sticky to touch.

5. Meanwhile, make the caramel. Measure the caster sugar and 2 tablespoons of water into a small stainless-steel saucepan. Stir over a medium heat until the sugar has dissolved and there are no crystals. Stop stirring and bring up to the boil. Boil until a golden caramel colour. Remove from the heat and carefully drizzle the caramel over the meringues using a spoon.

Lemon Queen of Puddings

This is an old-fashioned pudding but one I really love. Traditionally it was made with raspberry jam but I have replaced it with lemon curd as I love the combination of lemon and meringue.

Serves 6

600ml (1 pint)
   full-fat milk
25g (1oz) butter, plus
   extra for greasing
Finely grated zest
   of 1 lemon
225g (8oz) caster sugar
3 eggs, separated
75g (3oz) fresh white
   breadcrumbs
4 heaped tbsp
   lemon curd

**You will need a
1.4-litre (2½-pint)
shallow ovenproof
dish and a slightly
larger roasting tin.**

Mary's Tips

This is best made and baked straight away.

Not suitable for freezing.

1. Preheat the oven to 160°C/140°C Fan/Gas 3. Grease the ovenproof dish with butter.

2. Gently warm the milk in a small saucepan until hand hot. Add the butter, lemon zest and 50g (2oz) of the caster sugar. Stir until dissolved.

3. Lightly whisk the egg yolks in a bowl. Slowly pour the warm milk into the egg yolks, while whisking.

4. Sprinkle the breadcrumbs over the base of the buttered dish and pour the custard over the top. Leave to stand for about 15 minutes, so the breadcrumbs absorb the liquid.

5. Carefully transfer the dish to the roasting tin and fill the tin with hot water until it is halfway up the side of the dish. Bake in the preheated oven for about 25–30 minutes, until the custard has set. Remove from the oven and set aside to cool.

6. Reduce the oven temperature to 140°C/120°C Fan/Gas 1.

7. Whisk the egg whites in a large clean bowl using an electric whisk on full speed until they are like clouds. Add the remaining 175g (6oz) sugar, a teaspoon at a time, while whisking on maximum speed until the mixture is stiff and shiny.

8. Carefully spread the lemon curd on top of the set custard, then spread the meringue on top of the curd and create swirls. Return the pudding to the oven at the reduced temperature (not in the roasting tin of water) for about 30–35 minutes, until the meringue is pale golden all over and crisp.

9. Serve at once.

Rhubarb Plate Pie with Brandy Cream

A very old-fashioned pie made on an enamel or metal plate with a pastry top and bottom. My mother used to make a plate pie as a treat, piled high with fruit and sweet shortcrust pastry. Take note of the baking time and temperatures – preheat the oven to 200°C Fan, then lower to 160°C Fan after 15–20 minutes. This will give the perfect pie.

Serves 6

For the filling
650g (1lb 7oz) pink rhubarb, trimmed and cut into 2cm (¾in) slices (prepared weight)
125g (4½oz) caster sugar
4 tbsp cornflour

For the shortcrust pastry
2 eggs, beaten
350g (12oz) plain flour
225g (8oz) butter, cubed
55g (2oz) icing sugar

To glaze
2 tbsp caster sugar

For the brandy cream
300ml (½ pint) double cream
30g (1oz) icing sugar, sifted
2 tbsp brandy

You will need a 26cm (10¼in) enamel or metal plate.

1. To make the filling, measure the rhubarb, caster sugar and cornflour into a mixing bowl. Mix well until all the rhubarb is coated. Leave to stand at room temperature for about 30 minutes, until the cornflour and sugar have dissolved and coated the rhubarb. It should look glossy and not dry.

2. Meanwhile, to make the pastry, remove 3 tablespoons of the beaten eggs into a cup and set aside for later. Measure the flour and butter into a food processor. Whiz until breadcrumb stage. Stir in the icing sugar. Add the remaining beaten egg gradually and whiz until the pastry comes together. Tip out onto a lightly floured work surface and knead into a ball.

3. Divide the pastry, with one half just larger than the other (slightly more pastry is needed for the top of the pie). Set the larger half aside. Roll out the remaining pastry to a thinnish circle with a diameter about 6cm (2¼in) bigger than the base of the enamel plate. Line the plate with the pastry, leaving the excess overhanging.

4. Spoon the rhubarb mixture onto the middle of the plate, making a high peak in the centre. Brush the pastry edge with the egg wash.

Recipe continued

The pie is best to make and serve. Brandy cream can be made up to 2 days ahead.

Not suitable for freezing.

5. Roll out the remaining pastry on a lightly floured work surface to a large circle with a diameter about 10cm (4in) bigger than the plate. Carefully place the pastry over the filling and press down to seal the edges on the bottom piece of pastry. Trim around the edge using a sharp knife and reserve any trimmings for decoration. Using two fingers and thumb, crimp the edges to make a neat design. Using a small sharp knife, make a steam hole in the middle of the pie.

6. Roll out the trimmings on a lightly floured work surface and cut out large and small leaves. Brush the top of the pie with the reserved beaten egg and stick the leaves around the steam hole. Brush the top of the leaves with beaten egg and leave the pie to chill in the fridge for 30 minutes.

7. Preheat the oven to 220°C/200°C Fan/Gas 7 and place a heavy, flat baking sheet in the oven to get hot.

8. Sprinkle the pie with the caster sugar and place it on the hot baking sheet in the preheated oven. Bake for 15–20 minutes, then reduce the oven temperature to 180°C/160°C Fan/Gas 4 and continue to cook for about 30–35 minutes, until golden brown and the rhubarb is tender when a small knife is inserted into the pie. Leave to cool for 10 minutes.

9. Meanwhile, to make the brandy cream, whip the cream to soft peaks and stir in the sifted icing sugar and brandy. Chill in the fridge until needed.

10. Slice the pie into wedges and serve hot with the brandy cream on the side.

Apple and Lemon Steamed Pudding

**A steamed pudding is so comforting and this recipe is
great for using windfall apples in early autumn.**

Serves 6

225g (8oz) Bramley
apples, peeled and
diced (prepared
weight)

55g (2oz) butter,
melted, plus extra
for greasing

75g (3oz) light
muscovado sugar

150g (5oz) self-
raising flour

150g (5oz) baking
spread, straight
from the fridge

150g (5oz) caster sugar

2 eggs

1 tbsp milk

Finely grated zest
of 2 lemons

Golden syrup, warmed,
to serve (optional)

Mary's Tips

*Can be made up
to a day ahead.*

Freezes well.

1. Grease a 1.2-litre (2-pint) pudding basin with butter.

2. Mix the apples, melted butter and light muscovado sugar
   together in a bowl. Spoon into the base of the prepared basin.

3. Measure the flour, baking spread, caster sugar, eggs, milk and
   zest into a mixing bowl. Whisk together using an electric
   whisk until pale in colour and fluffy in texture. Spoon on top
   of the apples and level the top.

4. Place a large piece of tin foil on a work surface and arrange
   a piece of non-stick baking paper on top. Make a pleat in the
   middle and use to cover the pudding. Carefully seal the top
   by folding tightly or securing with string.

5. Put a trivet or an enamel plate in the base of a large saucepan.
   Place the basin on top and fill the saucepan with boiling
   water until halfway up the sides of the basin. Cover the pan
   with a lid and simmer for about 2–2½ hours, until well risen
   and the sponge is firm in the middle.

6. Remove the foil and paper and tip upside down onto a plate.
   Carefully remove the basin. Drizzle with some warmed
   golden syrup, to serve, if liked.

7. Serve with cream or custard.

Foolproof Custard

Although there are good ready-made custards available, this is such a foolproof recipe and it tastes so delicious, it's worth the time it takes to make.

600ml (1 pint)
  full-fat milk
3 egg yolks
25g (1oz) caster sugar
1 rounded tbsp
  cornflour
2 tsp vanilla extract
5 tbsp pouring double
  cream (optional)

Mary's Tips

Can be made up to 8 hours ahead, covered and kept warm or reheated to serve.

Not suitable for freezing.

1. Pour the milk into a saucepan and heat until just below boiling point.

2. In a bowl combine the yolks, caster sugar, cornflour and vanilla extract. Mix well to a smooth paste. Pour in the hot milk and whisk.

3. Clean the saucepan, then pour the custard through a sieve into the pan. Stir over a medium heat until the custard has thickened and coats the back of a spoon.

4. Stir in the double cream, if using, to make a richer custard.

Baking

Whole Lemon Sandwich Cake

There are two whole lemons used in the cake, icing and decoration, so the flavour is intense. A food processor is used to chop the cooked lemons, therefore it is easy to make the cake in the processor, too. There's no need to wash the processor after chopping the lemons.

Serves 8

For the cake

2 small thin-skinned lemons

275g (10oz) baking spread, straight from the fridge

275g (10oz) caster sugar

275g (10oz) self-raising flour

2 level tsp baking powder

4 eggs

For the filling and topping

300ml (½ pint) pouring double cream

165g (5½oz) luxury lemon curd

Icing sugar, sifted, to dust

Mary's Tips

Cake can be made a day ahead. Best iced on the day.

Cakes freeze well with filling.

1. Preheat the oven to 180°C/160°C Fan/Gas 4. Grease and base-line 2 × 20cm (8in) round loose-bottomed deep cake tins with non-stick baking paper.

2. Place the 2 whole lemons in a small saucepan, cover with water and bring to the boil. Reduce the heat and simmer for 20–30 minutes, or until very soft and tender. Drain and set aside to cool.

3. Cut the lemons in half and remove any pips. Place the halved lemons in a food processor (including the skins) and process until slightly smooth but with some chunky bits. Tip the mixture into a small bowl.

4. Add all the other cake ingredients to the unwashed food processor and blend until smooth. Lift out the blade and stir in just over half the lemon pulp. Divide the mixture evenly between the prepared tins and bake in the preheated oven for about 30 minutes, or until pale golden brown and just shrinking from the side of the tins. Leave to cool for 5 minutes, then turn out, peel off the paper and leave to finish cooling on a wire rack.

5. To make the filling, whip the cream until it holds its shape, then add the lemon curd and the remaining lemon pulp. Stir well.

6. Slice both cakes in half horizontally, using a serrated or bread knife, to make four layers. Divide the filling into three and use to sandwich the layers together. Dust the top of the cake with lots of icing sugar to serve.

Finnish Apple and Cinnamon Cake

**This recipe was inspired by a Finnish friend of mine. It is a
sponge, generously topped with apples and cinnamon.**

Serves 6

115g (4oz) baking
   spread, straight
   from the fridge
115g (4oz) self-
   raising flour
200g (7oz) caster sugar
2 large eggs
3 large Bramley apples,
   peeled and sliced
   into large chunks
   (485g/1lb 1oz
   prepared weight)
2 tsp ground cinnamon
2 tbsp nibbed sugar
   or 6 lumps of
   sugar, crushed

Mary's Tips

*Can be made up to
a day ahead and
reheated to serve.*

Freezes well.

1. Preheat the oven to 160°C/140°C Fan/Gas 3. Well grease
   the base and sides of a 20cm (8in) springform tin.

2. Measure the baking spread, flour, 115g (4oz) of the caster
   sugar and the eggs into a large bowl. Whisk using an electric
   whisk until smooth.

3. Spread half the cake mixture into the base of the prepared tin.
   Spread the remaining mixture halfway up the sides of the tin.

4. Coat the apples in the remaining caster sugar and the
   cinnamon, then place them in the centre of the cake mixture.
   Press into the sides. Sprinkle with the nibbed or crushed
   sugar and bake in the preheated oven for about 1½ hours,
   until well risen and golden.

5. Serve warm with custard or cream.

Christmas Stollen

This is a traditional German Christmas bread. Prove it in a warm place – an airing cupboard is ideal, or if you have a two-oven Aga, sit the baking sheet on a tea towel and put it on top of the simmering oven lid. I don't add currants, as I find they tend to burn easily.

Serves 8

225g (8oz) strong
   white flour
7g packet fast-action
   dried yeast
75g (3oz) very
   soft butter
½ tsp grated nutmeg
2 eggs
100ml (3½fl oz) milk
Oil, for greasing
55g (2oz) caster sugar
Zest of 1 lemon
175g (6oz) mixed dried
   fruit of your choice
   (e.g. raisins, sultanas)
175g (6oz) marzipan
Icing sugar, to dust

Mary's Tips

*It will keep for up to
1 week in an airtight
container in the fridge.*

Freezes well.

1. Cut a piece of non-stick baking paper to a rectangle that measures about 30 × 17cm (12 × 7in).

2. Measure the flour, yeast, butter and nutmeg into a large mixing bowl.

3. Crack one of the eggs into a jug and beat well. Add the milk and stir together.

4. Pour the egg and milk mixture into the bowl with the dry ingredients and mix together by hand, or in a free-standing mixer using a dough hook, until the dough has come together.

5. Tip out onto a lightly floured work surface and knead by hand for 10 minutes, or in the mixer for 5 minutes on a low speed, until the dough is soft, smooth and shiny. A slightly wet dough is best.

6. Place the dough in a lightly oiled bowl and cover with cling film. Leave to rise in a warm place for at least 2 hours, or until the dough has doubled in size and is light and puffy.

7. Tip the dough out onto a lightly floured work surface and knock back by hand, or in the mixer, then knead in the caster sugar, lemon zest and fruit until it is evenly distributed. Place the dough on the prepared non-stick baking paper and roll out to fit the rectangle.

Recipe continued

8. Roll the marzipan to a long sausage shape the same length as the dough. Lay the marzipan down one long side and roll up like a Swiss roll. Seal the edges by tucking the dough under and mould the roll into a long, thin loaf. Slide the paper and stollen onto a baking sheet, then cover with cling film or a large poly bag. Tie the ends so the bag creates a warm atmosphere. Leave to prove a second time in a warm place for about 30–45 minutes, or until it has doubled in size again.

9. Preheat the oven to 200°C/180°C Fan/Gas 6.

10. Remove the bag or cling film and discard. Beat the second egg and use it to glaze the surface of the stollen. Bake in the preheated oven for about 20–25 minutes, until light golden brown and the stollen sounds hollow when tapped underneath (check after 15 minutes: you may need to cover with foil, if the top is getting too brown).

11. Leave to cool on a wire rack, then dust heavily with icing sugar to serve.

Chocolate Oat Cookies

This is the biscuit you always want in the tin – oaty, chocolaty, gooey, golden and delicious! These are perfect to serve on the side with a dessert, as a special treat.

Makes 30

150g (5oz) butter

125g (4½oz) golden syrup

125g (4½oz) plain flour

25g (1oz) cocoa powder

175g (6oz) large old-fashioned porridge oats

75g (3oz) light muscovado sugar

1 tsp bicarbonate of soda

115g (4oz) plain chocolate chips

Mary's Tips

Can be made up to a day ahead.

The cookies freeze well unbaked and baked.

1. Preheat the oven to 200°C/180°C Fan/Gas 6. Line 2 large baking sheets with non-stick baking paper.

2. Melt the butter and syrup together in a large saucepan over a medium heat. Remove the pan from the heat and add the flour, cocoa powder, oats, sugar and bicarbonate of soda. Mix well with a wooden spoon and leave to cool.

3. Add the chocolate chips and mix again. Be careful not to add the chocolate chips while the mixture is still hot or they will melt. They are better kept whole when stirred into the mix, so they just melt gently in the oven.

4. Divide the mixture into 30 equal pieces, then roll each one into a ball. Place the balls on the prepared baking sheets and flatten them slightly with your hand, making sure you leave space for spreading. Bake in the preheated oven for about 15 minutes, until just firm to touch.

5. Leave to cool on the baking sheet for a few minutes, then transfer to a wire rack to cool completely.

Almond Snowballs

Impressive and delicious almond biscuits, these are like ratafia biscuits. It's important to use almond extract rather than essence – extract is just what it says, extracted from the nuts, so has a really good flavour.

Makes 16

2 egg whites
100g (3¾oz)
  caster sugar
175g (6oz) ground
  almonds
1 tsp almond extract
55g (2oz) blanched
  almonds, chopped
55g (2oz) icing
  sugar, sifted

Mary's Tips

*Can be made up
to a day ahead.*

Freeze well.

1. Line 2 large baking sheets with non-stick baking paper.

2. Place the egg whites in an electric mixer or large bowl and whisk on full speed until they look like clouds. Slowly add the caster sugar, a teaspoon at a time, until stiff and glossy.

3. Gently fold in the ground almonds, almond extract and chopped almonds until well incorporated (be careful not to knock any air out of the mixture). Chill in the fridge for 30 minutes to firm up.

4. Preheat the oven to 180°C/160°C Fan/Gas 4.

5. Place the icing sugar in a large bowl. Using wet hands, shape the mixture into 16 balls and coat in the icing sugar. Place on the baking sheets, leaving space for the balls to spread.

6. Bake in the preheated oven for about 20 minutes, until pale golden and a hard crust has formed. Remove from the oven and leave to cool on a wire rack.

Dairy-free Chocolate Cake

**After several goes at trying to make a really good, moist,
dairy-free chocolate cake, we think this is a winner.**

Serves 8

175g (6oz) self-
  raising flour
1 tsp baking powder
1 tsp bicarbonate of soda
2 tbsp cocoa
  powder, sifted
150g (5oz) caster sugar
2 eggs
2 tbsp golden syrup
150ml (¼ pint)
  sunflower oil, plus
  extra for greasing
160ml (5½fl oz)
  coconut cream
4 tbsp apricot
  jam, warmed
30g (1oz) dairy-free
  white chocolate,
  coarsely grated

For the icing
160ml (5½fl oz)
  coconut cream
3 × 85g bars dairy-free
  milk or dark chocolate,
  broken into pieces

Mary's Tips

Cakes freeze well uniced.

*Can be made and
assembled up to 6
hours ahead.*

1. Preheat the oven to 180°C/160°C Fan/Gas 4. Grease 2 × 20cm
    (8in) loose-bottomed sandwich tins and line the base with
    non-stick baking paper.

2. To make the cake, measure the flour, baking powder,
    bicarbonate of soda, cocoa powder and caster sugar into a bowl
    and mix well.

3. Place the eggs, syrup, oil and coconut cream in a jug and whisk
    to combine.

4. Pour the wet ingredients into the dry and whisk together using
    an electric whisk until well combined.

5. Divide the batter between the prepared tins and bake in the
    preheated oven for about 25–30 minutes, or until well risen
    and springing away from the sides of the tins. Remove from
    the oven, turn out on to a wire rack, peel off the baking paper
    and leave to cool.

6. Meanwhile, to make the icing, place the coconut cream
    and dairy-free chocolate in a bowl and melt over a pan of
    simmering water, taking care that the bottom of the bowl does
    not touch the water. Stir until runny. Set aside in a cool place
    or chill in the fridge until it is a thick spreading consistency.

7. Place one cake on a serving plate and spread half the apricot
    jam on top. Cover with half the icing, then sandwich the
    second cake on top. Cover with the remaining jam and icing.
    Swirl the icing in the centre of the cake.

8. Carefully sprinkle the white chocolate gratings around the edge
    of the cake to make a thick ring pattern. Cut into slices to serve.

Almond Loaf Cake

Delicious served as a cake or warm with custard or cream as a dessert.

150g (5oz) baking
spread, straight
from the fridge
225g (8oz) self-
raising flour
1 tsp baking powder
125g (4½oz)
caster sugar
1 tsp almond extract
55g (2oz) ground
almonds
2 tbsp milk
4 eggs
25g (1oz) flaked
almonds

Mary's Tips

*Can be made up
to a day ahead.*

Freezes well.

1. Preheat the oven to 160°C/140°C Fan/Gas 3. Grease and line a 900g (2lb) loaf tin with non-stick baking paper.

2. Measure all the cake ingredients except the flaked almonds into a mixing bowl. Whisk using an electric whisk for 2 minutes until pale, light and fluffy. Spoon into the tin and level the surface.

3. Sprinkle the flaked almonds on top and bake in the preheated oven for about 1½ hours until well risen and pale golden in colour. Test it is cooked through by inserting a skewer into the centre of the loaf. If it is clear, the cake is cooked. Leave to cool on a wire rack.

4. Remove the baking paper and cut into thick slices to serve.

Coffee and Mascarpone Cake

A rich and indulgent coffee cake with mascarpone coffee icing.

Serves 8–10

1 tbsp strong coffee
  granules
225g (8oz) self-
  raising flour
4 eggs
225g (8oz) baking
  spread, straight
  from the fridge
225g (8oz) caster sugar
2 level tsp baking
  powder
10g (¼oz) dark
  chocolate, grated

**For the mascarpone
icing**
1 level tbsp strong
  coffee granules
115g (4oz) butter,
  softened
225g (8oz) icing
  sugar, sifted
250g (9oz) full-fat
  mascarpone cheese

Mary's Tips

*Can be made up
to a day ahead.*

Freezes well iced.

1. Preheat the oven to 180°C/160°C Fan/Gas 4. Grease and base line 2 × 20cm (8in) sandwich tins with non-stick baking paper.

2. To make the cake, measure the coffee granules into a large mixing bowl. Pour in 2 tablespoons of very hot water and stir to dissolve. Add the flour, eggs, baking spread, caster sugar and baking powder to the bowl. Whisk using an electric whisk for about 2 minutes until light and fluffy.

3. Divide between the prepared tins and level the tops. Bake in the preheated oven for about 25–30 minutes until well risen and springing away from the sides of the tins. Turn out and leave to cool on a wire rack.

4. To make the icing, measure the coffee granules into a large mixing bowl. Pour in 2 tablespoons of very hot water and stir to dissolve. Add the butter and icing sugar and whisk with an electric whisk until light and airy. Add the mascarpone and whisk again until smooth and creamy.

5. Once the cakes have cooled, remove the paper and sandwich together using half the icing. Spread the remaining icing on top and swirl. Sprinkle with the grated chocolate to serve.

Lazy Days Raspberry Cake

This cake is a genoise cake, which originates from Genoa in Italy and is one of my most favourite cakes. It is slightly more technical than other cakes, as it has whisked egg whites and melted butter, but this gives a very light and airy sponge.

Serves 8

4 large eggs, separated
125g (4½oz)
   caster sugar
1 tsp vanilla extract
40g (1½oz) butter,
   melted
125g (4½oz) self-
   raising flour

For the filling
300ml (½ pint) pouring
   double cream
2 tbsp icing sugar,
   sifted, plus extra
   to finish
200g (7oz) raspberries

Mary's Tips

Cakes can be made up to 8 hours ahead. Assemble up to 6 hours ahead.

Cakes freeze well.

1. Preheat the oven to 180°C/Fan 160°C/Gas 4. Grease a 20cm (8in) deep round cake tin and line the base and sides with non-stick baking paper.

2. Measure the egg yolks and sugar into a bowl and whisk with an electric whisk until pale and light in texture. When the whisks are lifted from the mixture they should form a trail. Add the vanilla and gradually pour in the melted butter, mixing carefully. Gradually sift in the flour, mixing carefully until smooth and combined.

3. In a separate bowl, whisk the egg whites with an electric whisk until they form soft peaks. Fold the egg whites into the cake mixture until evenly blended (being careful not to knock the air out of the mixture).

4. Turn into the prepared tin and bake in the preheated oven for about 30–35 minutes, or until well risen and pale golden brown. Leave to cool in the tin for a few minutes then turn out, peel off the paper and finish cooling on a wire rack.

5. To make the filling, whisk the cream until it holds its shape, then stir in the sifted icing sugar. Mix half the whipped cream with half of the raspberries.

6. Cut the cake in half horizontally using a serrated or bread knife. Place one half on a cake stand and spread the raspberry cream over the cake base. Top with the other half sponge, then spread the remaining cream on top. Arrange the remaining raspberries standing up on top of the cream.

7. Dust with icing sugar just before serving.

Conversion
Chart
and Index

———

Weights

Metric	Imperial
5g	⅛oz
10g	¼oz
15g	½oz
20g	¾oz
25/30g	1oz
35g	1¼oz
40g	1½oz
55g	2oz
60g	2¼oz
65g	2½oz
75g	3oz
80g	3¼oz
90g	3½oz
115g	4oz
125g	4½oz
150g	5oz
165g	5½oz
175g	6oz
200g	7oz
225g	8oz
250g	9oz
275g	10oz
300g	10½oz
325g	11½oz
350g	12oz
360g	12½oz
375g	13oz
400g	14oz
425g	15oz
450g	1lb
500g	1lb 2oz
525g	1lb 3oz
550g	1¼lb

Metric	Imperial
600g	1lb 5oz
650g	1lb 7oz
675g	1½lb
700g	1lb 9oz
750g	1lb 10oz
800g	1¾lb
850g	1lb 14oz
900g	2lb
1kg	2lb 4oz
1.25kg	2lb 12oz
1.3kg	3lb
1.5kg	3lb 5oz
1.7kg	3lb 12oz
1.8kg	4lb
2kg	4lb 7oz
2.25kg	5lb

Oven Temperatures

°C	Fan °C	°F	Gas Mark
120	100	250	½
140	120	275	1
150	130	300	2
160	140	325	3
180	160	350	4
190	170	375	5
200	180	400	6
220	200	425	7
230	210	450	8
240	220	475	9

Volume

Metric	Imperial
30ml	1fl oz
50ml	2fl oz
75ml	2½ fl oz
85ml	3fl oz
100ml	3½fl oz
125ml	4fl oz
150ml	5fl oz (¼ pint)
175ml	6fl oz
200ml	7fl oz (⅓ pint)
225ml	8fl oz
240ml	8½fl oz
250ml	9fl oz
275ml	9½fl oz
300ml	10fl oz (½ pint)
350ml	12fl oz
400ml	14fl oz
450ml	15fl oz (¾ pint)
500ml	18fl oz
600ml	20fl oz (1 pint)
700ml	1¼ pints
750ml	1¼ pints
900ml	1½ pints
1 litre	1¾ pints
1.2 litres	2 pints
1.25 litres	2¼ pints
1.5 litres	2½ pints
1.75 litres	3 pints
1.8 litres	3¼ pints
2 litres	3½ pints
2.25 litres	4 pints
2.5 litres	4½ pints
2.75 litres	5 pints
3.4 litres	6 pints
3.9 litres	7 pints
4.5 litres	8 pints (1 gallon)

Measurements

Metric	Imperial
5mm	¼in
1cm	½in
1.5cm	5/8in
2cm	¾in
2.5cm	1in
3cm	1¼in
4cm	1½in
5cm	2in
6cm	2¼in
6.5cm	2½in
7cm	2¾in
7.5cm	3in
9cm	3½in
10cm	4in
11cm	4½in
12.5cm	5in
15cm	6in
16cm	6½in
18cm	7in
20cm	8in
23cm	9in
25cm	10in
28cm	11in
30cm	12in
33cm	13in
35cm	13¾in
36cm	14in
40cm	15¼in
46cm	18in

Big Thank Yous

Writing this book has been a sheer pleasure. The Home Team have excelled themselves; they are loyal, dedicated and creative. Lucy Young is certainly in charge; after 35 years being by my side, she has the highest of standards and sorts everything. The recipes have to look amazing and tempting and, of course, taste delicious. We set out a plan together and, along with Lucinda McCord, we test all the recipes at home until they are foolproof and guaranteed to be successful for everyone making them at home. We love what we do and laugh lots, too. Our always willing tasters Kathryn, Allison and Paul, my husband, prefer the classic recipes, whereas our children, Tom and Annabel, are more adventurous, they enjoy modern trends and flavours. Their young try everything and keep us on our toes!

From the publishers, thank you to Albert DePetrillo for commissioning the book and for his wonderful upbeat weekly emails! Thanks to Phoebe Lindsley, editor holding the fort in-house, and Jo Roberts-Miller, our editor for over 20 years, who knows the way we work and whose two sons benefit as tasters, too! Designer Abi Hartshorne has worked on our last four books and does a wonderful job.

On the food photography book shoot, photographer Tara Fisher, home economist the wonderful Lisa Harrison, Isla Murray and Alice Hughes, and props stylist Sophie Louise Robinson, thank you for testing and creating the stunning photos for the book. We are lucky to have the Dream Team.

The Glam Squad – Jo Penford, for hair, make-up and general loveliness, and Tess Wright, for styling and finding wonderful clothes for me to wear – they are our dream team and we are so grateful for their dedication to us.

Our guardian angels – literary agent Caroline Wood, who guides us and is a joy to work with, and our media agents, Joanna Kaye and Theia Nankivell, who hold our hands and completely understand us.

Thank you to all our readers for your amazing support.

I work because I love it, and the people I work with give me the greatest joy, so thank you all.

Mary Berry

BBC Books, an imprint of Ebury Publishing
One Embassy Gardens, 8 Viaduct Gdns,
Nine Elms, London SW11 7BW

BBC Books is part of the Penguin Random House group of companies
whose addresses can be found at global.penguinrandomhouse.com

Penguin
Random House
UK

Photography by Tara Fisher

First published by BBC Books in 2024

www.penguin.co.uk

A CIP catalogue record for this book is available from the British Library

ISBN 9781785949227

Publishing Director: Albert DePetrillo
Editor: Phoebe Lindsley
Project Editor and Copyeditor: Jo Roberts-Miller
Food Stylist: Lisa Harrison
Prop Stylist: Sophie Louise Robinson
Design: Hart Studio
Production: Antony Heller

The authorised representative in the EEA is Penguin Random
House Ireland, Morrison Chambers, 32 Nassau Street, Dublin D02 YH68.

Printed and bound in Germany by Mohn Media Mohndruck GmbH

Penguin Random House is committed to a sustainable future for
our business, our readers and our planet. This book is made
from Forest Stewardship Council® certified paper.